स्वादिष्ट
लंच-डिनर

कलात्मक ढंग से स्वादिष्ट व्यंजन बनाने की विधि

लेखिका
आशारानी व्होरा

संशोधन/अनुवाद
सीमा गुप्ता

वी एण्ड एस पब्लिशर्स

प्रकाशक

वी एण्ड एस पब्लिशर्स

F-2/16, अंसारी रोड, दरियागंज, नई दिल्ली-110002

☎ 23240026, 23240027 • फैक्स: 011-23240028

E-mail: info@vspublishers.com • *Website:* www.vspublishers.com

क्षेत्रीय कार्यालय : हैदराबाद

5-1-707/1, ब्रिज भवन (सेन्ट्रल बैंक ऑफ इण्डिया लेन के पास)

बैंक स्ट्रीट, कोटी, हैदराबाद-500 095

☎ 040-24737290

E-mail: vspublishershyd@gmail.com

शाखा : मुम्बई

जयवंत इंडस्ट्रिअल इस्टेट, 1st फ्लोर-108, तारदेव रोड

अपोजिट सोबो सेन्टर, मुम्बई – 400 034

☎ 022-23510736

E-mail: vspublishersmum@gmail.com

फ़ॉलो करें:

DISCLAIMER

इस पुस्तक में सटीक समय पर जानकारी उपलब्ध कराने का हर संभव प्रयास किया गया है। पुस्तक में संभावित त्रुटियों के लिए लेखक और प्रकाशक किसी भी प्रकार से जिम्मेदार नहीं होंगे। पुस्तक में प्रदान की गयी पाठ्य सामग्रियों की व्यापकता या सम्पूर्णता के लिए लेखक या प्रकाशक किसी प्रकार की वारंटी नहीं देते हैं।

पुस्तक में प्रदान की गयी सभी सामग्रियों को व्यावसायिक मार्गदर्शन के तहत सरल बनाया गया है। किसी भी प्रकार के उद्धरण या अतिरिक्त जानकारी के स्रोत के रूप में किसी संगठन या वेबसाइट के उल्लेखों का लेखक या प्रकाशक समर्थन नहीं करता है। यह भी संभव है कि पुस्तक के प्रकाशन के दौरान उद्धृत बेवसाइट हटा दी गयी हो।

इस पुस्तक में उल्लिखित विशेषज्ञ के राय का उपयोग करने का परिणाम लेखक और प्रकाशक के नियंत्रण से हटकर पाठक की परिस्थितियों और कारकों पर पूरी तरह निर्भर करेंगा।

पुस्तक में दिये गये विचारों को आजमाने से पूर्व किसी विशेषज्ञ से सलाह लेना आवश्यक है। पाठक पुस्तक को पढ़ने से उत्पन्न कारकों के लिए पाठक स्वयं पूर्ण रूप से जिम्मेदार समझा जायेगा।

उचित मार्गदर्शन के लिए पुस्तक को माता-पिता एवं अभिभावक की निगरानी में पढ़ने की सलाह दी जाती है। इस पुस्तक के खरीददार स्वयं इसमें दिये गये सामग्रियों और जानकारी के उपयोग के लिए सम्पूर्ण जिम्मेदारी स्वीकार करते हैं।

इस पुस्तक की सम्पूर्ण सामग्री का कॉपीराइट लेखक/प्रकाशक के पास रहेगा। कवर डिजाइन, टेक्स्ट या चित्रों का किसी भी प्रकार का उल्लंघन किसी इकाई द्वारा किसी भी रूप में कानूनी कार्रवाई को आमंत्रित करेंगा और इसके परिणामों के लिए जिम्मेदार समझा जायेगा।

मुद्रक: रेप्रो नॉलेजकास्ट लिमिटेड, ठाणे

प्रकाशकीय

भारतीय गृहिणी अब वह सदियों पुरानी गृहिणी नहीं, जो घंटों कमर झुकाये, अधगीली लकड़ियों से चूल्हा फूँकती, आँखें मलती रसोईघर के नाम पर धुएँ वाली काली कोठरी में घुटती हुई अपनी आधी जिन्दगी बिता देती थी। जिसका उद्देश्य पेट के माध्यम से पति का मन जीतना भर होता था। भीतरी जनानखाने से खाना भेजने के अलावा जिसका मेहमानों से कोई सीधा सम्पर्क नहीं होता था।

अब वह एक जागरूक गृहिणी है, समाज का एक उपयोगी अंग है। विज्ञान और तकनीक की दुनिया ने उसके घर के भीतर की तकलीफदेह दुनिया भी बदली है। वह स्वयं भी बदलते समय के साथ कदम मिलाकर चलना चाहती है। वैज्ञानिक साधनों, तकनीकी ढंग और अपने कलात्मक स्पर्श से अपने काम को बेहतर ढंग से करना चाहती है तथा श्रम और समय की बचत कर, अपने बचे समय को, बची शक्तियों को अन्य उपयोगी कामों में भी लगाने की इच्छा रखती है। वह जानती है, यदि नहीं जानती तो जानना चाहती है कि आज उसका काम जैसे-तैसे भोजन पकाना ही नहीं है, इस कला में बेहतर ढंग से पारंगत होना भी है। भोजन-सम्बन्धी आवश्यक जानकारी, रसोई की सुघड़ व्यवस्था, स्वच्छता से पकाना और कलात्मक ढंग से सजाकर परोसना, मेहमानों के स्वागत-सत्कार का आधुनिक शिष्टाचार, ये सभी बातें इस प्रशिक्षण में आती हैं। जो गृहिणी जितनी अधिक इस कला-विज्ञान में प्रशिक्षित होती है, वह घर-बाहर से उतनी ही अधिक प्रशंसित होती है।

पाक कला और व्यंजन विधियों पर बाजार में और भी कई पुस्तकें उपलब्ध हैं। पर यह पुस्तक उनसे भिन्न है और अपने ढंग की हिन्दी में पहली व अकेली पुस्तक है।

किन मायनों में?

प्रस्तुत पुस्तक में अन्य पुस्तकों की तरह साग-भाजी, अचार चटनी से लेकर मुरब्बा मिठाई तक की विधियाँ मात्र नहीं लिखी गयी हैं, शहर से कस्बे तक की हर गृहिणी की समस्या हल की गयी है। यही नहीं, राष्ट्रीय भावात्मक एकता के प्रसार के लिए और अन्तर्राष्ट्रीय बिरादरी में शामिल होने के लिए आज जिस मिले-जुले स्वाद वाले मीनू पर जोर दिया जाता है, पुस्तक में इस अछूते विषय पर भी सुन्दर ढंग से लिखा गया है और इस सुन्दरता, विविधता, विशिष्टता को मुखर करते हैं, अनेकों सम्बन्धित चित्र, जिनकी सहायता से मेज-सज्जा और प्लेटों की सज्जा को समझने में आसानी होगी।

महिला प्रशिक्षण-केन्द्रों की अनुभवी व्यवस्थापिका और महिलोपयोगी तकनीकी विषयों को विख्यात लेखिका की जादुई कलम से विशिष्ट व्यंजन-विधियों और उनकी विशिष्ट सज्जा से सम्बन्धित यह पुस्तक कैसी बन पड़ी है, कितनी उपयोगी है, इसका निर्णय पाठिकाएँ स्वयं ही कर सकेंगी।

दो दशक से यह पुस्तक प्रकाशित की जा रही है, किन्तु अब दोबारा इसका संशोधित व परिवर्द्धित संस्करण आम पाठकों की सुविधा, विषय की नवीनता आदि के दृष्टिकोण से प्रकाशित किया जा रहा है, जो पाक-कला प्रेमी हमारी महिला पाठिकाओं के लिए अधिक उपयोगी साबित होगी।

प्रस्तावना

फलाँ ऐसा भोजन बनाती है... इस सफाई और सुघड़ता से पकाती है... इस सलीके से परोसती है कि जी चाहता है, उसकी उँगलियाँ चूम लें। सचमुच उसके हाथों में स्वाद का जादू है।

गाहे-बगाहे ऐसी तारीफें आपने भी सुनी होंगी और उन पर रश्क (ईर्ष्या) भी किया होगा।

शायद यह कहावत भी सुनी हो, 'मेहमान की प्रशंसा और पति की प्रीति उनके पेट के माध्यम से पाइये।' पर यह कहावत शायद अब पुरानी पड़ चुकी है। आज पेट और आँखों के माध्यम को समान महत्त्व मिल गया है। भोजन का स्वाद और उसका आकर्षण का पलड़ा-लगभग बराबर हो गया है।

भोजन कितना ही स्वादिष्ट हो, पौष्टिक हो, यदि उसकी प्रस्तुति ऐसी नहीं है कि खाने वालों को वह प्लेट, अपने आकर्षण में बाँध सके या परोसने वाले हाथों की स्वागत-कला से अभिभूत कर सके, तो उस पर किया गया खर्च व मेहनत सार्थक नहीं ही माना जायेगा। भोजन से तृप्ति के साथ पकवानों की एक भाषा भी चाहिए, उनकी प्रस्तुति में एक अभिव्यक्ति भी होनी चाहिए, एक आमन्त्रण भी चाहिये। प्रशंसात्मक प्रतिक्रियाएँ, पकवान-प्लेटों की यह प्रस्तुति ही आमन्त्रित करती है।

हो सकता है, आप अच्छा भोजन बनाना जानती हों, पर भोजन की किस्म, उसे बनाने में सफाई-स्वच्छता का ध्यान, पकाने की सही विधि ताकि भोजन के आवश्यक गुणों की रक्षा हो सके, इस पर खाने वालों की रुचियों के साथ उसकी अनुकूलता, परोसने का आकर्षक ढंग-ये सारी ही बातें मिलकर आपकी पाक-कला का परिचय देंगी।

कुछ स्वादिष्ट नास्ते को तैयार करने और उन्हें खुशनुमा ढंग से सजाकर घर के सदस्यों एवं मेहमानों के सामने परोसने की कला सिखाने वाली यह पुस्तक इसी मायने में पाक-कला की अन्य पुस्तकों से भिन्न है।

विषय-सूची

लंच/डिनर - शाकाहारी सूप.................9
टमाटर सूप.................9
मिश्रित सब्जियों का सूप.................10
लंच/डिनर - माँसाहारी सूप.................11
जापानी मिजूटाकी सूप.................11
मटन सूप.................12
लंच/डिनर - स्टार्टर और तन्दूरी.................13
ग्रीक चीज़ रोल्स.................13
स्ट्रिंग हॉपर.................14
चीज़ स्टार्ज़.................15
पनीर टिक्का.................16
माछेर चाप.................17
फ्राइड पेम्फ्रेट मछली.................18
तन्दूरी मुर्ग.................19
शामी कबाब.................20
सींक कबाब.................21
कीमा-बड़ा.................22
आलू कीमा पैटीज.................23
चमत्कारी मटन चाप.................24
लंच/डिनर - विशिष्ट शाकाहारी व्यंजन....25
तिरंगी सब्जी.................25
गोभी मुसल्लम.................26
भरवा टमाटर.................27
परवल की नावें.................28
दही में बनी कश्मीरी मिर्चें.................29
वेजीटेबल कीमा.................30
पालक-पनीर.................31
खोये-काजू की सब्जी.................32

साई भाजी.................33
हरियाली मक्खनी पनीर.................34
कश्मीरी दम आलू.................35
कड़ाही पनीर.................36
मलाई कोफ्ता.................37
चिकन करी.................38
लंच/डिनर - माँसाहारी व्यंजन.................39
रोगन जोश.................39
कीमा-कोफ्ता करी.................40
गोआनी लिवर करी.................41
चिकन मक्खनी.................42
लंच/डिनर - रोटियाँ.................43
नान.................43
मिस्सी रोटी.................44
रूमाली रोटी.................45
लच्छा परांठा.................46
लंच/डिनर - चावल के व्यंजन.................47
पुलाव.................47
मुगलई बिरियानी.................48
अण्डे-टमाटर वाले चावल.................49
स्पेनिश राइस.................50
लंच/डिनर - दही के व्यंजन.................51
दहीबड़ा.................51
बथुये का रायता.................52
फ्रूट रायता.................53
सलाद ड्रेसिंग.................54
लंच/डिनर - सलाद.................55
फ्रेंच ड्रेसिंग.................55

सलाद की नाव.........................56

गुलदस्ते के रूप में सलाद.....................57

सलाद-सज्जा.........................58

लंच/डिनर – मिठाइयाँ 59

मिठाई दिलबहार 59

तिरंगी टिक्की 60

छेना मुरगी 61

कोकोनट बरफी 62

रस बड़ा 63

मूँग की बरफी.........................64

शाही टोस्ट 65

गाजर का हलवा 66

सूजी का हलवा 67

आइसक्रीम 68

कुल्फी 69

फ्रूट कस्टर्ड 70

फ्रूट क्रीम 71

पोटैटो चॉकलेट पुडिंग 72

टमाटर सूप

टमाटर का सूप जायकेदार व पौष्टिक होता है।

टमाटर सूप

सामग्री

250 ग्राम टमाटर
2 कप पानी
2 चम्मच चीनी
2 बड़ी इलायची
¼ चम्मच काली मिर्च
2 चम्मच मक्खन
नमक (स्वादानुसार)

विधि

ढाई सौ ग्राम अच्छे लाल टमाटर लेकर उन्हें टुकड़ों में काटिए। दो कप पानी, थोड़ा नमक, दो चम्मच चीनी, एक बड़ा कतरा हुआ प्याज, दो मोटी इलायची, ¼ छोटी चम्मच पिसी हुई काली मिर्च डालकर पकाइये। टमाटर, प्याज गलकर घुलने लगें, तो उतारकर, मसलकर स्टेनलेस स्टील की छलनी से या जाली के साफ कपड़े से छानिए। अब पतीली में दो चम्मच मक्खन गरम कीजिए। मन्दी आँच पर इसमें एक चम्मच मैदा भूनिए। फिर छना हुआ रस डालकर पाँच मिनट पकाइए। सूप तैयार है। इसे गरम-गरम ही प्यालों में डालकर परोसना चाहिए। परोसते समय ऊपर से डबलरोटी के छोटे टुकड़े तलकर डाल सकती हैं। इन्हें पहले से डालकर नहीं रखना चाहिए।

कुछ टिप्स

पकने के बाद सूप में कुछ तुलसी के पत्ते डाल कर ढक दें। इससे सूप में एक खास खुशबू आ जाती है।

मिश्रित सब्जियों का सूप

इस सूप में विभिन्न प्रकार की सब्जियाँ डाल कर इसे और स्वादिष्ट बना सकते हैं।

मिश्रित सब्जियों का सूप

सामग्री

2 टमाटर

2 गाजर

2 पत्ते सहित हरे प्याज

पालक की एक छोटी गड्डी

2 या 3 पत्ते बन्दगोभी के

1 छोटी मूली पत्तों सहित

½ कप उबले हुए मटर

½ चुकन्दर

1-2 हरी मिर्च

हरा धनिया

3-4 पत्ते पुदीने के

काली मिर्च

मक्खन

नमक (स्वादानुसार)

विधि

सभी सब्जियों को पहले साफ पानी में धोलें। फिर छोटे-छोटे टुकड़ों में काट लें। नमक, काली मिर्च, इलायची, पानी में डालकर कुकर में पकाइए कि सभी सब्जियाँ अच्छी तरह गल जायें और भाप में पकने पर उनके विटामिन भी सुरक्षित रहें। प्रेशर के दस मिनट बाद कुकर उतार कर ठण्डा करें। फिर सब्जियों को मसलकर सूप छान लें। अब पतीली में तीन-चार चम्मच मक्खन गरम कर उसमें डेढ़ दो चम्मच मैदा मन्दी आँच पर भूनिए। फिर छना हुआ सूप डालकर दो बड़ी चम्मच चीनी मिलाइए और पतीली को ढककर दस मिनट तक पकाइए। प्यालों में डालकर उसी तरह गरम परोसिए।

कुछ टिप्स

पकने के बाद सूप में कुछ तुलसी के पत्ते डालकर ढक दें। इससे सूप में एक खास खुशबू आ जाती है।

जापानी मिज़ू टाकी सूप

जापानी भोजन सादा और पौष्टिक होता है।

मिज़ूटाकी सूप

सामग्री

8-10 टुकड़े मुर्गी का गोश्त
1 कप कटा हुआ पत्तागोभी
1 कप कटी हुई बींस
1 कप कटी हुई गाजर
बीस मशरूम
1 चम्मच सोया सॉस
1 कप राइस नूडल्स
नमक (स्वादानुसार)

विधि

साथ का चित्र देखिए। जापानी मिज़ूटाकी सूप बनाने के लिए यह स्पेशल चिमली वाला बरतन प्रयोग में लाया जाता है। इसके नीचे कोयले जलाकर ऊपर पानी भर लिया जाता है। इस खौलते पानी में मुर्गी के छोटे-छोटे टुकड़े व नमक डालकर पहले लगभग दस मिनट पकने दीजिए। टुकड़े तीन चौथाई गलें, पूरी तरह बन्द गोभी, गाजर, फ्रेंचबीन, मशरूम डालिए। कुछ अन्य सब्जियाँ सूप में डालनी हों, तो वे भी टुकड़े करके डाल दीजिए। अब तक टेबल पर रखने के लिए कोयलों की आँच मन्दी हो जानी चाहिए। अन्त में जरा-सी सोयाबीन सॉस और थोड़ी राइस नूडल्स भी इस सूप में डाल दीजिए और मन्दी आँच पर पकता हुआ यह सूप चिमनी वाले बरतन में ही भोजन की मेज पर ले जाइए।

कुछ टिप्स

मिज़ूटाकी सूप को एक खास बरतन में पकाया जाता है और उसी से परोसा जाता है।

मटन सूप

यह सूप ताकत और जायके में लाजवाब है।

मटन सूप

सामग्री

250 ग्राम मीट
2 प्याज
1 गाजर
½ चम्मच चीनी
1 अण्डा
½ चम्मच सौंफ
4 लौंग
2 बड़ी इलायची
नमक (स्वादानुसार)
मक्खन

विधि

गोश्त के टुकड़े साफकर व धोकर पतीली में डालिए। गाजर, प्याज के टुकड़े, इलायची, लौंग, अजवाइन नमक डालकर पकाइए। ढककर मन्दी आँच पर दो घण्टे पकाना चाहिए। फिर उतारकर मसलिए व छान लीजिए। सूप बिल्कुल साफ दिखे, इसके लिए एक अण्डे की सफेदी को झागदार होने तक फेंटिए। इसे थोड़ा गरम कीजिए (उबालना नहीं है), फिर कपड़े से छानकर सूप में मिला दीजिए। पतीली में दो छोटी चम्मच मक्खन गरम कीजिए। उसमें आधी चम्मच चीनी भूनकर सुर्ख (लाल) कीजिए। चाहें तो कुछ मटर के दाने भी इसमें तल सकती हैं। सूप डालकर मन्दी आँच पर पाँच मिनट फिर पकाइए। भुनी चीनी से रंग सुर्ख हो जायेगा। प्याले में डालकर परोसते समय टोस्ट के टुकड़े डाल सकती हैं।

कुछ टिप्स

यह सूप अत्यन्त पौष्टिक एवं स्वादिष्ट होता है।

ग्रीक चीज़ रोल्स

यदि इस व्यंजन को शाकाहारी रूप में बनाना चाहें, तो इसकी भरावन में गोश्त न मिलायें।

चीज़ रोल्स

सामग्री

1 कप मैदा
3 बड़े चम्मच किसा हुआ पनीर
¼ छोटा चम्मच नमक
1 चम्मच घी
150 ग्राम उबले हुए आलू
½ कप कीमा
2 मध्यम प्याज
½ कप किसा हुआ पनीर
1 बड़ा चम्मच बूस्टर सॉस
हरा धनिया
नमक
कतरी हुई हरी मिर्च

विधि

मैदे में नमक मिलाकर छानिए। किसा हुआ पनीर और 1 चम्मच घी मिलाइए। बर्फ वाले ठण्डे पानी का छींटा देकर गूँथिये। फिर फ्रिज में घण्टे भर तक रख दीजिए। उसके बाद निकालकर दोबारा मसलिए व 15-16 गोलियाँ बना लीजिए।

भराव के लिए उबले आलू छीलकर कुचलिए। इसमें किसा हुआ पनीर मिलाइए। कतरा हुआ हरा धनिया और नमक भी मिला लीजिए।

प्याज कतर कर फ्राईपैन में घी गरम कर उसमें भूनिए। जब लाल हो जायें, तो कतरी हुई हरी मिर्च और एक बड़ी चम्मच बूस्टर सॉस मिलाइए। फिर उबला हुआ कीमा मिलाकर भूनिए। नमक डालकर उतार लीजिए। एक कड़ाही में घी गरम कीजिए। तैयार आटे की एक गोली पूरी की तरह बेलिए। आलू मिश्रण चम्मच में लेकर पूरी पर फैलाइए इसके ऊपर भुना हुआ कीमा फैलाइए और पूरी को गोल-लपेट लीजिए। मैदे के घोल से खुले किनारे बन्द कीजिए। इन्हें 'टूथपिक्स' से भी बन्द कर सकती हैं, फिर एक-एक रोल कड़ाही में छोड़कर तल लीजिए।

कुछ टिप्स

मिजूटाकी सूप को एक खास बर्तन में पकाया जाता है और उसी से परोसा जाता है।

स्ट्रिंग हॉपर की बनावट मोमो जैसे होती है, परन्तु स्वाद अलग होता है।

स्ट्रिंग हॉपर

सामग्री

1 कप चावल का आटा
250 ग्राम कीमा
100 ग्राम आलू
100 ग्राम प्याज
3 हरी मिर्च
1 नींबू
1 छोटी चम्मच गरम मसाला
¼ छोटी चम्मच राई
¼ छोटी चम्मच खसखस
¼ छोटी चम्मच जीरा
4 कलियाँ लहसुन
¼ छोटी चम्मच कुटी हुई सौंफ
2 बड़ी चम्मच टमाटर सॉस
नमक और घी अन्दाज से

विधि

एक कप चावल के आटे को पौन कप उबलते पानी में थोड़ा-थोड़ा करके डालिए। एक चुटकी नमक छोड़कर जल्दी-जल्दी चलाइए व उतार लीजिए। ठण्डा होने पर मसलकर भीगे कपड़े से लपेटकर रख लीजिए। थोड़ी देर बाद फिर मसलकर इस आटे की छोटी छोटी गोलियाँ बनाइए। एक छोटा केक मोल्ड लेकर उसमें (या बड़ी कड़ाही में ही) रखकर एक-एक गोली को भीगे हाथ से दबाइए और छोटी छोटी कटोरियाँ-सी (केक-मोल्ड की तरह) बना लीजिए। एक बड़ी पतीली में उबलते पानी पर छलनी रखकर इन्हें भाप में पका लीजिए।

अब कड़ाही में घी डालकर आधे प्याज कतर कर भूनिए। कतरी हुई हरी मिर्च, पिसी हुई खसखस, सौंफ, राई, जीरा छोड़िए। पिसा हुआ लहसुन डालकर थोड़ा भूनिए, फिर कीमा छोड़िए। नमक व आधा कप पानी डालकर पकाइए। कीमा गल जाये, पानी सूख जाये तो फिर मन्दी आँच पर भूनिए। आधा नींबू निचोड़िए और गरम मसाला मिलाकर उतार लीजिए।

शेष आधे प्याज को चकलियों में काटिए और घी में तलकर निकाल लीजिए। आलू छीलकर कद्दूकस कीजिए। इन्हें भी घी में तलकर निकाल लीजिए व थोड़ा नमक मल लीजिए।

चावल के आटे के पके मोल्ड (कटोरियाँ) रखिए। हर मोल्ड में पहले भूना हुआ कीमा रखिए। इस पर तले प्याज की चकलियों में से एक-एक मोटा छल्ला जमाइए व उसमें जले आलुओं का किस भरिए। टमाटर सॉस से ऊपर धारियाँ बनाइए।

कुछ टिप्स

चावल का आटा हर बड़े डिपार्टमेण्टल स्टोर में मिलता है। आप चाहें तो घर में ही सूखे चावल के दाने पीस कर भी यह आटा बना सकती हैं।

चीज़ स्टार्ज़

चीज़ स्टार बेहद स्वादिष्ट एवं सेहतमन्द डिश हैं।

चीज़ स्टार्ज़

सामग्री

4 चम्मच कार्नफ़्लोर

4 बड़े चम्मच मक्खन/सलाद का तेल

4 चम्मच आटा

6 चम्मच किसा हुआ पनीर

1 अण्डा

नमक (स्वादानुसार)

लाल मिर्च (स्वादानुसार)

काली मिर्च (स्वादानुसार)

विधि

आटा और कार्नफ्लोर मिलाकर छानिए। सलाद का तेल या मक्खन मिलाकर कस लीजिए। पनीर और मसाले मिलाइए। अण्डा तोड़कर उसकी केवल जर्दी मिलाइए और मसलिए। यदि आटा सख्त लगे, तो एक डेढ़ चम्मच दूध मिलाकर मुलायम कर लीजिए। चकले पर रोटी की तरह बेलिए और चाकू से बरफी की तरह चौकोर टुकड़ियाँ काटिए या किसी गोल ढक्कन से गोल बिस्कुटों की तरह काट लीजिए।

बेकिंग ट्रे को मक्खन लगाकर चिकना कीजिए। ये कटी टुकड़ियाँ उस पर रखकर ओवन में मन्दी आँच पर बेक कीजिए। चाय के साथ गरमा-गरम परोसिए।

कुछ टिप्स

हर चीज़ स्टार को पार्सल, धनिया और गोल प्याज के टुकड़ों से सजाइए।

पनीर टिक्का

पनीर टिक्का गरमागरम परोसा जाये, तो उसका स्वाद बेहतरीन होता है।

पनीर टिक्का

सामग्री

500 ग्राम पनीर

1 प्याज

1 शिमला मिर्च

1 टमाटर

कुछ मशरूम

धनिया पत्ती बारीक कटी हुई

मेरीनेट करने के लिए:

½ कप सादा दही

1 चम्मच लहसुन का पेस्ट

1 चम्मच अदरक का पेस्ट

2 चम्मच तन्दूरी मसाला

1 चम्मच भुना हुआ जीरा

2 चम्मच चाट मसाला

लाल मिर्च (स्वादानुसार)

नमक (स्वादानुसार)

विधि

पनीर के ½" लम्बे टुकड़े काट लें। सभी सब्जियाँ भी चकोर टुकड़ों में काट लें। इन सब सब्जियों को एक साथ मेरीनेट करके पेस्ट में मिलाकर रख दें। पनीर के टुकड़ों पर भी मेरीनेट पेस्ट लगाकर तीन घण्टों के लिए फ्रिज में रखें। बारबेक्यू की डण्डियों पर पनीर और सब्जियाँ लगाकर अच्छी तरह तन्दूर में सेंक लें। फिर प्लेट में निकाल कर सलीके से सजायें। परोसने से पहले हरा धनिया नींबू के टुकड़े भी उसपर डालें।

कुछ टिप्स

तन्दूरी पनीर टिक्के हरी चटनी के साथ परोसें। खाने का मजा दोगुना हो जायेगा।

माछेर चाप

मछली की खास गन्ध न आने के कारण मछली के चॉप सब पसन्द करते हैं।

माछेर चाप

सामग्री

250 ग्राम मछली

175 ग्राम आलू

2 मध्यम प्याज

1 अण्डा

½ कटोरी डबलरोटी का चूरा

1 चम्मच चीनी

अदरक, लहसुन, नमक, मिर्च,
गरम मसाला, घी (अन्दाज से)

विधि

आलू उबालिए व छीलकर मसलिए। मछली काटकर उबालिए। उबलते समय पानी में एक चम्मच नमक छोड़िए। गल जाने पर काँटे निकालकर मछली कुचलिए। एक प्याज बारीक लम्बी कतरनों में काटिए। दूसरा प्याज, अदरक, लहसुन पीस लीजिए। कटा हुआ प्याज घी में, लाल मिर्च व पिसा मसाला मिलाकर मन्दी आँच पर घी अलग छोड़ने तक भूनिए। मछली डालिए। पाँच मिनट तक भूनकर उतारिए। आलुओं में नमक, मिर्च, कतरा हुआ हरा धनिया मिला कर इनकी लोइयाँ बनाइए। आलू के इस पेड़े के बीच मछली भरकर लम्बी टिकिया बनाइए। एक चपटी व गहरी प्लेट में अण्डा फेंट लीजिए। इसमें मछली-आलू की यह टिकिया डुबोकर निकालिए, डबलरोटी के चूरे में लपेटिए और घी में तल लीजिए। माछेर चाप या मछली के चाप तैयार हैं।

कुछ टिप्स

मछली को घी की जगह सरसों के तेल में भी तल सकते हैं।

फ्राइड पेम्फ्रेट मछली

इस मछली में अधिक काँटे नहीं होते हैं, इसलिए यह अत्यन्त स्वादिष्ट लगती है।

फ्राइड पेम्फ्रेट मछली

सामग्री

एक मध्यम आकार की पेम्फ्रेट
मछली
1 कप दही
1 नींबू
2 प्याज
अदरक, नमक, मिर्च, हल्दी,
गरम मसाला, घी (अन्दाज से)

विधि

मछली साफ करके साबुत रखिए व उसे बीच-बीच से चाकू से गहरे चीरे लगा दीजिए। प्याज, अदरक पीसिए। दही में सब मसाले डालकर मछली में भरिए व एक घण्टा रख दीजिए। फिर खुले घी में उलट-पुलटकर तल लीजिए, पहले तेज व फिर मन्दी आँच पर इतना पकाइए कि गल जाये और कुरकुरी हो जाये। ऊपर से नींबू निचोड़ सकती हैं। नींबू निचोड़कर गरम मसाला व कटा हुआ धनिया छिड़क लीजिए।

कुछ टिप्स

एक बड़ी प्लेट में पूरी फ्राइड पेम्फ्रेट मछली रखिए। मछली के आकार की एक दूसरी चपटी प्लेट में माछेर चाप रखिए और मछली के आकार का फूलदान साथ में सजा दीजिए। मेहमानों के लिए आकर्षण सज्जा के साथ मछली के ये दो स्वादिष्ट व्यंजन आपके मेज की शोभा बढ़ायेंगे।

तन्दूरी मुर्ग

तन्दूरी चिकन को अच्छी तरह भूनने से उसका स्वाद बढ़ जाता है।

तन्दूरी मुर्ग

सामग्री

1 मध्यम आकार की मुर्गी
2 चम्मच नींबू का रस
4 चम्मच दही
½ चम्मच काला जीरा
2 इलायची
घी, प्याज, लहसुन, अदरक, नमक,
मिर्च, गरम मसाला (अन्दाज से)

विधि

अदरक, लहसुन, प्याज एक साथ पीस लें। दही में मिलाकर घोल बना लें। यह घोल मुर्ग के ऊपर व भीतर अच्छी तरह लेप कर दें। पाँच मिनट तक रखकर सूखने दें। अब नींबू के रस में पिसा हुआ जीरा, मिर्च, नमक मिलाकर मुर्ग के सब ओर खाँचे लगाकर उनमें भर दें। फिर इसे एक घण्टे तक रख दें। कबाब वाले सींखचे में पिरोकर ऊपर से घी मल दें, फिर तन्दूर में भून लें। पक जाने पर कतरा हुआ धनिया व गरम मसाला छिड़ककर परोसें।

कुछ टिप्स

नींबू, प्याज और सलाद के साथ तन्दूरी मुर्ग और भी स्वादिष्ट लगेगा।

शामी कबाब

शामी कबाब को भारी तली के बर्तन में तल सकते हैं या ओवन में भून भी सकते हैं।

शामी कबाब

सामग्री

2 कप चने की दाल
250 ग्राम कीमा
1 बड़ा प्याज
2 हरी मिर्च
3 लहसुन की कलियाँ
½ इंच टुकड़ा अदरक
¼ चम्मच नींबू का
पिसा हुआ छिलका
¼ चम्मच जीरा
4 लौंग
¼ चम्मच पिसी हुई दालचीनी
¼ चम्मच पिसी हुई काली मिर्च
हरा धनिया नमक, घी (अन्दाज से)

विधि

चने की दाल को रातभर भिगोकर रखिए। सुबह जरा दरदरी पीस लीजिए। प्याज, लहसुन, अदरक, हरा धनिया, हरी मिर्च बारीक कतरिए। नींबू के छिलके के अलावा सारे मसाले कीमा में मिलाकर फेंटिए। दालपीठी भी मिला लीजिए। बड़े नींबू के बराबर गोलियाँ बनाइए। नींबू का पिसा हुआ छिलका बीच में रखकर गोलियों को लम्बाई में रोल कर लीजिए। इन्हें गरम घी में सुर्ख होने तक तल लीजिए। प्याज, खीरे, टमाटर या चटनी के साथ परोसिए।

कुछ टिप्स

आप शामी कबाब को अपने मनपसन्द आकार में बना सकती हैं।

सींक कबाब

सींक कबाब केवल बकरे के गोश्त के भी बनाये जा सकते हैं।

सींक कबाब

सामग्री

250 ग्राम मुर्गे व बकरे के गोश्तों का
कीमा समान भागों में मिलाकर

1 नींबू

1 चम्मच खसखस

2 मोटी इलायची

4 लौंग

¼ चम्मच दालचीनी चूर्ण

1 चम्मच पिसा हुआ धनिया

½ चम्मच पिसी हुई लाल मिर्च

¼ चम्मच पिसी हुई काली मिर्च

2 मध्यम आकार के प्याज

लहसुन, हरी मिर्च, हरा धनिया,
नमक व घी (अन्दाज से)

विधि

प्याज व लहसुन पीसिए। घी में भूनकर लाल मिर्च, धनिया, इलायची, लौंग, खसखस व दालचीनी का चूर्ण मिलाइए। कीमा, कतरा हुआ हरा धनिया, हरी मिर्च, लाल व काली मिर्च, नमक व नींबू का रस मिलाइए। थोड़ा उलट-पुलट कर उतार लीजिए। लोहे की सींक पर घी चुपड़ कर इस मिश्रण को सींक कर चढ़ाकर कबाब बनाइए। फिर सींक को कोयलों की मन्दी आँच पर भूनिए। बीच-बीच में साफ कपड़े के टुकड़े लेकर घी चुपड़ती जाइए। भुन कर सुर्ख हो जायें, तो निकालकर गरम-गरम परोसिए। सलाद और चटनी के साथ बहुत स्वादिष्ट लगेंगे।

कुछ टिप्स

सींक कबाब को पतली रूमाली रोटी में लपेट कर भी खा सकती हैं।

कीमा-बड़ा

कीमा बड़ा नमकीन होते हैं, मीठे नहीं।

कीमा–बड़ा

सामग्री

250 ग्राम कीमा

125 ग्राम बेसन

1 बड़ा प्याज

2 हरी मिर्च

¼ चम्मच लाल मिर्च

¼ चम्मच गरम मसाला

1 इंच का टुकड़ा अदरक

अमचूर, हरा धनिया, नमक, घी

(अन्दाज से)

विधि

कीमा धोकर कुकर में डालिए। चुटकी भर नमक डालकर पकाइए। प्रेशर आने के एक मिनट बाद उतार लीजिए। निकालकर ठण्डा कीजिए। इसमें बेसन, कतरी हुई हरी मिर्च, हरा धनिया, महीन कतरा हुआ प्याज व अदरक, मिलाइए। लाल मिर्च, गरम मसाला, अमचूर व नमक मिलाकर छोटी-छोटी गोलियाँ बनाइए। इन्हें चपटाकर आलू की टिकियों की तरह तवे पर घी डालकर तलिए। मन्दी आँच पर देर तक तलकर सुर्ख करना चाहिए। कड़ाही में घी डालकर भी तल सकती हैं। फिर निकालकर सलाद व चटनी के साथ परोसिए।

कुछ टिप्स

कीमा बड़ा बनाने के लिए मुर्गे या बकरे का गोश्त प्रयोग कर सकते हैं।

आलू कीमा पैट्रीज

प्याज के बने फूलों से इन पैट्रीज की प्लेट को सजायेंगे, तो वह बहुत सुन्दर लगेगी।

आलू कीमा पैट्रीज

सामग्री

250 ग्राम कीमा

250 ग्राम आलू

1 अण्डा

½ कप सूखी डबलरोटी का चूरा

2 मध्यम प्याज

नमक, मिर्च, कतरी हुई हरी मिर्च,
हरा धनिया, गरम मसाला,
एक नींबू, घी अन्दाज से

विधि

आलू उबालकर छीलिए। कुचलिए। कड़ाही में घी डालकर महीन कतरे हुए प्याज भूनिए। कीमा डाल कर भूनिए, फिर थोड़ा पानी व नमक डालकर इसे गला लीजिए। पानी इतना ही हो कि बचे नहीं। अब कीमा को फिर मन्दी आँच पर भूनिए व गरम मसाला कतरी हुई हरी मिर्च, हरा धनिया डालिए। आधे नींबू का रस मिलाकर उतार लीजिए।

कुचले हुए आलुओं में शेष आधा नींबू निचोड़िए। नमक, लाल मिर्च व हरा धनिया मिलाइए। आलू की अखरोट के बराबर गोलियाँ बनाइए। हाथ से खोखली कर भीतर मसाले वाला भुना कीमा भरिए और फिर गोलकर पैट्टी को बारी-बारी अण्डे के घोल में डुबोकर डबलरोटी के चूरे में लपेटिए और घी में तल लीजिए।

सज्जा: इन्हें सूप और सलाद के साथ परोसिए या पहले सूप देकर बाद में सलाद व चटनी के साथ पैट्टीज मेज पर लाइए। चित्र में देखिए - सलाद में प्याज के बने फूल। ये फूल किसी भी सलाद के साथ सजा सकती हैं। हरे प्याजों को कलियों के रूप में चीरा लगाकर पानी में उलटा करके भिगो दीजिए। दो-तीन घण्टे बाद प्याज के फूलों की कलियाँ खिलने लगेंगी। इन्हें थोड़ी डण्डी छोड़कर काटिए और छोटी शीशियों के कण्टेनर्स में सजा दीजिए। शेष सलाद-सज्जा आप अपनी पसन्द अनुसार करें।

कुछ टिप्स

अधिक तले भोजन से परहेज करने वाले इस पैटी को भून कर भी खा सकते हैं।

चमत्कारी मटन चाप

चाप की प्लेट को तीन उबले आलुओं से बने वेटर गुड्डे से सजायें। तीनों आलू एक के ऊपर एक रखकर गुड्डा बनायें और उसके मुँह पर लौंग, टमाटर और खीरे से आँख, नाक आदि बनायें।

मटन चाप

सामग्री

6 लम्बी बड़ी चापें

2 प्याज

250 ग्राम आलू

1 अण्डा

2 बड़े टमाटर

2 लौंग

बड़ी इलायची

1 इंच का टुकड़ा अदरक का

6 कलियाँ लहसुन की

½ कप सिरका

½ कप सूखी डबलरोटी का चूरा

काली मिर्च, घी, नमक, लाल मिर्च (अन्दाज से)

विधि

चापों को धोकर साफ कीजिए। प्याज को बारीक कतर लीजिए। लहसुन अदरक पीस लीजिए। चापों को पिसा हुआ मसाला मिलाकर दो घण्टे के लिए सिरके में भिगो दीजिए। सिरके से निकालकर इतने पानी के साथ कुकर में पकाइए कि चापें गल जायें और पानी न बचे या कम से कम बचे। कुकर ठण्डा होने पर चापें निकालिए। आलू उबालकर छीलिए व कुचलिए। कुचले हुए आलू में टमाटर का गूदा, नमक, लाल, काली और हरी मिर्च, कतरा हरा धनिया, बारीक कतरे प्याज, पिसा हुआ गरम मसाला मिलाइए। अब इस मिश्रण को चापों के खाली हिस्सों में दबाकर भरिए। चापों की पतली हड्डियों की डण्डियाँ एक ओर बाहर निकली रहें। शेष चाप को आलुओं से आकार दीजिए। अब अण्डा फोड़कर फेंटिए। इसमें चुटकी भर नमक मिलाइए और दोबारा इतना फेंटिए कि झागदार हो जाये। सभी चापों को पहले अण्डे के इस घोल में डुबोइए, डबलरोटी के चूरे में लपेटिए और कड़ाही में गरम किये खुले घी में उलट-पुलट कर तल लीजिए।

कुछ टिप्स

उस वेटर-गुड़िया के होठों के बीच एक छोटी-सी अगरबत्ती सिगार की तरह लगा दें।

तिरंगी सब्जी

इस तिरंगी डिश को गाजर के छोटे-छोटे फूलों से भी सजा सकते हैं।

तिरंगी सब्जी

सामग्री

1 कटोरी मूँग की धुली हुई दाल
1 कटोरी हरी मटर के दाने
पनीर इसी अन्दाज से
1 गाजर
हरी मिर्च, नमक, मिर्च,
हल्दी व घी आवश्यकतानुसार।

विधि

दाल को इतने पानी में पकाइए कि गलने पर पानी पूरा सूख जाये। पकते समय इसमें नमक, हल्दी तथा लाल मिर्च छोड़िये। पक जाने पर इसे निकालकर कड़ाही में छौंकिए और थोड़ा भूनकर निकाल लीजिए। छौंकते समय थोड़ी हल्दी घी में डाल लेनी चाहिए ताकि रंग अच्छा पीला हो जाये।

मटर के दाने कूटिए। हरी मिर्च भी साथ ही कूट लीजिए। कड़ाही में थोड़ा घी गरम करके कुटे हुए मटर छौंकिए। थोड़ा पानी का छींटा और नमक डालकर पकाइए। नरम हो जाने पर मन्दी आँच पर भूनकर जरा सूखा कर लीजिए। पनीर में नमक और थोड़ा नींबू का रस मिलाकर खूब मसलिए। फिर इसे अलग छौंक लगाकर जरा भून लीजिए। अब आपके पास तीन रंग की चीजें तैयार हैं—पीली दाल, हरी मटर और सफ़ेद पनीर।

एक चपटी डिब्बी या कटोरदान में पहले जरा-सा घी चुपड़िए। अब इसपर पनीर की तह जमाइए। पहले मटर की व फिर दाल की। हाथ से दबाकर समतल करके रख दीजिए। थोड़ी देर बाद सेट हो जाने पर डिब्बी को प्लेट में औंधा कीजिए। तिरंगी सब्जी तैयार है। आप इन तीनों रंगों को ऊपर नीचे भी कर सकते है।

कुछ टिप्स

तीन रंग की एक ऐसी सब्जी, जो प्रोटीन से भरपूर होने के कारण पौष्टिक भी है।

गोभी मुसल्लम

गोभी आप सीजन-भर बनाती हैं। इस बार इसे जरा इस रूप में भी बनाकर देखिए, विशेष रूप से मेहमानों के लिए। स्वादिष्ट होने के साथ मेज पर यह प्लेट-सज्जा बहुत अच्छी लगेगी।

गोभी मुसल्लम

सामग्री

मध्यम आकार का अच्छा खिला
हुआ गोभी का फूल
4 प्याज
2 टमाटर
4 हरी मिर्च
हरा धनिया
मसाले
अदरक
लहसुन
सजाने के लिए सलाद पत्ती
तलने के लिए घी/तेल

विधि

गोभी का डण्ठल व पत्ते काटकर अलग कर दीजिए। फूल को साबुत ही धोकर जरा सुखा लीजिए। ऊपरी भाग नरम होता है, उस पर पौनी से उछालकर घी छोड़ती जाइए। जब हल्की लाल होने लगे, तो निचोड़ कर निकाल लीजिए।

अतिरिक्त घी कटोरी में निकाल कर थोड़े घी में प्याज, लहसुन, अदरक का पिसा हुआ मसाला भूनिए। सुर्ख हो जाने पर छिले हुए टमाटर के टुकड़े डालिए और मन्दी आँच पर कुछ देर पकाइए। हल्दी व लाल मिर्च पहले छोड़िए तथा नमक और गरम मसाला बाद में मसाला भुन जाने पर अब यह मसाला उतारकर प्लेट में रखी गोभी के मध्य अच्छी तरह भर दीजिए, फिर पाँच मिनट मन्दी आँच पर ढक कर दोबारा गोभी को पका लीजिए।

अब प्लेट में सलाद पत्ती बिछाइए (गोभी के नरम पत्ते भी बिछा सकती हैं)। मध्य में गोभी का यह मसाले वाला फूल सीधा रखिए और कतरे हुए हरे धनिए से सजाइए।

कुछ टिप्स

डण्ठल वाला भाग नीचे रहने से गोभी ठीक
गलेगी। ऊपरी भाग नरम होता है।

भरवाँ टमाटर

टमाटर आप सब्जी में डालती हैं। इन्हें अलग से इस तरह भरवाँ बनाकर भी देखिए। मेहमानों के लिए एक विशेष सब्जी के रूप में और प्लेट-सज्जा की दृष्टि से भी अच्छी रहेंगे।

भरवाँ टमाटर

सामग्री

8 मध्यम आकार के टमाटर
250 ग्राम आलू
मसाले
हरी मिर्च
हरा धनिया
घी
। चम्मच मैदा

विधि

टमाटरों को पहले धोकर पोंछ लें। अब इनके ऊपरी भाग से एक-एक छोटी चकली काटिए। भीतर का गूदा सावधानी से खुरच कर निकाल लीजिए व चकलियों के ढक्कन भी सम्भालकर रख लीजिए। आलू उबालकर छीलिए। कुचल कर उसमें टमाटर का गूदा मिलाइए। कटी हुई हरी मिर्च, लाल मिर्च, गरम मसाला, हल्दी, हरा धनिया भी मिला लीजिए। इस मिश्रण को टमाटरों के भीतर भरकर ऊपर चकलियों के ढक्कन लगाइए। मैदा पानी में गाढ़ा घोलिए, इसमें चुटकी भर नमक मिलाकर इससे ढक्कनों के छेद बन्द कीजिए।

कड़ाही में इतना घी डालिए कि टमाटर डूब सकें। तेज आँच पर जल्दी से तलकर निकाल लीजिए। टमाटर टूटें नहीं। पक जाने पर सावधानी से निकालने चाहिए।

अब चार-चार टमाटर दो प्लेटों में सजा दें। इनके ढक्कन उतारिए और खुले भाग पर कटा हुआ हरा धनिया बुरक दीजिए। सुन्दरता और स्वाद दोनों दृष्टियों से यह प्लेट पसन्द की जायेगी।

कुछ टिप्स

गलने लायक कोई चीज है ही नहीं, इसलिए आँच मन्दी करने की जरूरत नहीं, इससे टमाटर टूटकर आलू बिखर सकते हैं।

परवल की नावें

परवल यों भी एक स्वास्थ्यवर्द्धक सब्जी है। यदि इसे सुन्दर रीति से बनाकर सजायें, तो जो इसे पसन्द नहीं करते वे भी करने लगेंगे और उन्हें गुणकारी सब्जी का लाभ भी मिल सकेगा।

परवल की नावें

सामग्री

8 दाने परवल
2 टमाटर
2 प्याज
मसाले
। टुकड़ा मूली का
घी

विधि

परवल धोकर पोंछिए। मध्य से चीर कर दो टुकड़े कीजिए। घी गरम करके पहले तेज व फिर मन्दी आँच पर तलकर निकाल लीजिए।

प्याज का मसाला पीसकर घी में भूनिए। हल्दी व लाल मिर्च छोड़िए। टमाटर का गूदा छोड़कर भूनिए। अब अन्दाज से पानी छोड़कर जरा गाढ़ा रसा पका लीजिए। नमक और गरम मसाला डालकर रसे को पाँच मिनट मन्दी आँच पर रखिए।

लम्बी प्लेट में रसा पलटिए और उसमें (चित्र देखिए) नावों की कतार की तरह परवल के तले हुए टुकड़े जमा दीजिए। इन नावों पर मूली के पतले तिकोने टुकड़ों की पाल खड़ी कीजिए। रसे में तैरते परवल नदी में तैरती नावों जैसा समाँ बाँध देंगे।

कुछ टिप्स

परवल की नावें तरी में कुछ ऐसे प्रतीत होती हैं
जैसे नदी में नाव तैर रहे हों।

दही में बनी कश्मीरी मिर्चें

छोटे आकार की कश्मीरी मिर्चों को इस प्रकार भी बनाकर देखिए, शायद आपको पसन्द आयेंगी।

दही में बनी कश्मीरी मिर्च

सामग्री

8 छोटी मिर्चें
1 कटोरी दही
मसाले
घी
थोड़ा-सा पनीर

विधि

मिर्चों को धोकर आधा-आधा काटिए। गरम घी में तेज आँचपर तलकर निकाल लीजिए। दही को कपड़े में बाँधकर टाँगिए। पानी निचुड़ जाने पर निकालकर उसमें हल्दी, नमक, मिर्च (लाल मिर्च जरा-सी हों) मिलाए। अब यह मिश्रण मिर्चों के भीतर अच्छी तरह दबाकर भर दें। फिर मन्दी आँच पर ढककर पकाएँ। उतार कर प्लेट में सजायें और कद्दूकस किये हुए पनीर और कटे हुए हरे धनिये के मिश्रण से सजायें।

वेजीटे बल कीमा

शाकाहारी मेज पर भी कुछ चीजें ऐसी परोसी जा सकती हैं, जो माँसाहारी व्यक्तियों को वैसी सन्तुष्टि दे सकें और शाकाहारियों को खाने पर आपत्ति भी न हो। गोभी मुसल्लम के बाद अब ऐसी ही एक प्लेट और लीजिए-वेजीटेबल कीमा।

वेजीटेबल कीमा

सामग्री

1 मध्यम आकार की गोभी
4 प्याज
1 इंच का टुकड़ा अदरक
8-10 कलियाँ लहसुन की
2 टमाटर
मसाले
मूली, गाजर के टुकड़े
घी

विधि

गोभी को साबुत ही धोकर सुखा लीजिए। कद्दूकस कीजिए। प्याज, लहसुन, अदरक पीसिए। घी जरा ज्यादा डालकर मसाला भूनिए। प्याज लाल हो जाने पर टमाटर का गूदा व मिर्च डालकर भूनिए। अब कतरी हुई गोभी डालिए तथा ऊपर से नमक छोड़िए। गोभी को मन्दी आँचपर ढककर पकाइए। अधिक गलने न पाये। कीमे की तरह भूनकर उतार लीजिए।

प्लेट में पलटिए। गरम मसाला और कटा हुआ हरा धनिया छिड़किए। फिर चित्र के अनुसार मूली और गाजर के फूलों से सजा लीजिए।

कुछ टिप्स

सोयाबीन से भी आप इसी तरह 'वेजीटेबल कीमा' तैयार कर सकती हैं। कीमे जैसे आकार में सोयाबीन क्रिस्टल्स का डिब्बा बाजार में उपलब्ध है। बनाने से पूर्व उन्हें 15 मिनट पानी में भिगोना चाहिए।

पालक-पनीर

उत्तर भारतीय व्यंजनों में पालक-पनीर एक ऐसी भाजी है, जिसे स्वाद और खाद्य गुणों से भरपूर होने के कारण अब सभी जगह पसन्द किया जाता है।

पालक पनीर

सामग्री

½ किलो पालक

200 ग्राम पनीर

1 बड़ा टमाटर

1 प्याज

4 कली लहसुन

अदरक 1 छोटा टुकड़ा

नमक (स्वादानुसार)

मिर्च (स्वादानुसार)

विधि

पालक को साफकर पहले धो लीजिए, फिर काटिए। प्याज, लहसुन व अदरक पीस लीजिए। टमाटर छीलकर उसे भी काट लीजिए। पनीर के तिकोने या चौकोने छोटे टुकड़े काटकर उन्हें घी में तलिए व गुलाबी लाल होने पर निकालकर अलग रख लीजिए।

कुकर में पालक, अन्दाज से थोड़ा पानी व नमक डालकर प्रेशर आने के बाद पाँच मिनट तक पकाइए। पानी आधी कटोरी से ज्यादा नहीं बचना चाहिए। इस पानी को छानकर अलग रख लीजिए और पालक को सिलबट्टे पर महीन पीस लीजिए। अब घी में पहले प्याज लाल कीजिए, फिर अदरक, लहसुन, टमाटर, लाल मिर्च डालकर थोड़ी देर मसाला और भूनिए। अब पिसी हुआ पालक और तला हुआ पनीर मिलाकर चलाइए और पालक से निकाला गया पानी भी मिलाकर इसे थोड़ा पतला कर लीजिए। पाँच मिनट मन्दी आँच पर रखकर उतार लीजिए। पनीर की कुछ टुकड़ियाँ ऊपर भी सजाइए।

कुछ टिप्स

पालक पनीर एक बहुत ही स्वादिष्ट एवं लोकप्रिय उत्तर भारतीय व्यंजन माना जाता है और विशेष अवसरों, त्योहारों, आदि में बनाया जाता है।

खोये – काजू की सब्जी

यह एक महँगी, पौष्टिक और गरिष्ट भाजी है, जिसे विशेष मेहमानों के लिए विशिष्ट सब्जी के तौर पर ही प्रायः बनाया जाता है। सौंफ, इलायची से इसे जायकेदार और पाचक बनाकर पकाइए।

खोये काजू की सब्जी

सामग्री

200 ग्राम खोया

100 ग्राम काजू

50 ग्राम किशमिश

2 प्याज

5 कली लहसुन

1 इंच टुकड़ा अदरक का

1 बड़ा टमाटर

1 बड़ी चम्मच सौंफ

3 मोटी इलायची

नमक, हल्दी, लाल मिर्च, हरा धनिया, गरम मसाला (अन्दाज से)

विधि

काजू को इतने पानी में एक उबाल दीजिए जिसमें कि वे केवल डूब सकें। फिर पानी छानकर काजू अलग कर लीजिए। किशमिश साफ कीजिए। सौंफ व इलायची दाना कूट लीजिए। प्याज के पतले लच्छे कतरिए। अदरक, लहसुन पीसिए, हरा धनिया कतरिए।

कड़ाही में घी डालकर प्याज के लच्छे भूनिए। हल्के लाल हो जाने पर अदरक, लहसुन की पेस्ट मिलाइए। थोड़ा और भूनकर हल्दी, लाल मिर्च, टमाटर का गूदा व काजू उबालकर बचा पानी मिलाइए। पाँच मिनट तेज आँच पर पकाने के बाद मन्दी आँच पर मसाला तब तक भूनिए, जब तक कि घी अलग न छोड़ने लगे। पाँच मिनट तेज आँच पर पकाने के बाद सौंफ इलायची व नमक मिलाइए और मन्दी आँच पर ढककर पकाइए। पाँच मिनट बाद कतरा हुआ हरा धनिया और गरम मसाला छिड़ककर उतार लीजिए। प्लेट को फिर काजू-दानों से सजाइए।

कुछ टिप्स

इस डिश को ज्यादा नहीं खा सकते हैं, इसलिए
इसे पकाते समय यह बात ध्यान रखें।

साई भाजी

खनिज लवणों-विटामिनों से भरपूर कई सब्जियों और प्रोटीन से भरपूर चने की दाल को मिलाकर बनायी जाने वाली यह पौष्टिक स्वादिष्ट भाजी एक लोकप्रिय सिन्धी व्यंजन है। आप भी बनाकर देखिए।

साई भाजी

सामग्री

100 ग्राम चने की दाल

200 ग्राम पालक

1 मुट्ठी मेथी

1 गुच्छी चुका या खट्टी भाजी

1 बैंगन

1 टुकड़ा कद्दू

गोभी

1 मध्यम आकार का आलू

1 गाजर

1 टमाटर

2 प्याज

5–6 कलियाँ लहसुन

1 टुकड़ा अदरक

2–3 हरी मिर्च

हल्दी, पिसा हुआ धनिया, नमक (अन्दाज से)

विधि

चने की दाल को एक कप पानी के साथ कुकर में चढ़ायें। प्रेशर आने के दो मिनट बाद कुकर आँच से उतार लें। सभी सब्जियाँ धोकर काट लें। कुकर ठण्डा होने पर खोलकर ये सारी सब्जियाँ और मसाले मिलाकर पहले की अधपकी दाल में डाल दें। कुकर बन्दकर प्रेशर के बाद फिर पाँच मिनट तक पकने दें। इसके बाद सभी सब्जियाँ व दाल को एक साथ घोंट दें। कड़ाही में घी डालकर पिसे हुए प्याज, लहसुन, अदरक का मसाला भूनें। फिर घोंटी हुई दाल-सब्जी मिलाकर चला दें। तीन मिनट मन्दी आँच पर ढककर पकायें, फिर निकालकर मूली-पत्ती और किसे हुए पनीर के साथ सजायें व चावल के साथ परोसें।

कुछ टिप्स

खट्टी भाजी न मिल सकें, तो थोड़ा इमली घोलकर उसका पानी बाद में मिला लें।

हरियाली मक्खनी पनीर

इस डिश में पनीर का स्वाद और शिमला मिर्च की खुशबू है।

हरियाली मक्खनी पनीर

सामग्री

250 ग्राम पनीर
1 चम्मच नींबू का रस
1 चम्मच हरी मिर्च का पेस्ट
1 चम्मच अदरक
नमक (स्वादानुसार)
6 टमाटर
1 चम्मच तेल
4 लहसुन की कलियाँ (कटी हुई)
1 कटी हुई शिमला मिर्च
4 छोटे प्याज बारीक कटे हुए
4 चम्मच मक्खन
5 लौंग
3 छोटी इलायची
1 टुकड़ा दालचीनी
3 बड़े चम्मच खोया
1 चम्मच गरम मसाला
½ कप ताजी क्रीम
½ चम्मच कसूरी मेथी

विधि

टमाटर को पीस लें। पनीर के टुकड़ों को नींबू के रस, मिर्च के पेस्ट और नमक में मेरीनेट कर लें। कड़ाही में तेल लें। उसमें लहसुन का पेस्ट, शिमला मिर्च और प्याज डालकर चलायें। ठण्डा होने पर पीसकर पेस्ट बना लें। एक बर्तन में मक्खन गरम करें। इसमें लौंग, इलायची, दालचीनी डालकर चलायें। इसमें अदरक लहसुन का पेस्ट भी डालें। अब खोया और टमाटर का पेस्ट डालकर चलायें। थोड़ा गरम मसाला, शहद और नमक डालकर मिलायें। इसमें पनीर के टुकड़े डालें। ताजी क्रीम और कसूरी मेथी डालकर चलायें और गरमागरम परोसें।

कुछ टिप्स

इस व्यंजन में पालक की दो-तीन पत्तियाँ पीस कर डालने से सब्जी का रंग चटकदार हरा हो जाता है।

कश्मीरी दम आलू

आलू की सब्जी बनाने के अनेक तरीकों में से यह सबसे ज्यादा प्रचलित है।

कश्मीरी दम आलू

सामग्री

900 ग्राम आलू
नमक (स्वादानुसार)
तलने के लिए घी या तेल
1 बड़ी प्याज (बारीक कटी हुई)
12 लहसुन की कलियाँ
2 चम्मच अदरक
4 चम्मच पिसा हुआ टमाटर, 140 मि.ली.
दही
1 हरी मिर्च
1 चम्मच गरम मसाला
(4 लौंग, 4 तेज पत्ता, 6 काली मिर्च, 4 छोटी
इलायची, 1 बड़ी इलायची, 1 टुकड़ा दालचीनी)
1 चम्मच खसखस
1 चम्मच धनिया
1 चम्मच जीरा
2 साबुत लाल मिर्च
1 चम्मच हल्दी
चुटकी भर जायफल और जावित्री

विधि

आलू रगड़कर छील लें और उन्हें काँटे से गोद दें। फिर इन आलुओं को हल्के नमक मिले पानी में 2 घण्टों के लिए भिगो दें। पानी से निकालकर आलू कपड़े से सुखा लें और कड़ाही में तेल डाल कर सुनहरा होने तक तल लें।

एक बर्तन में घी गरम करके उसमें कटी हुई प्याज भून लें। सभी मसाले भी साथ ही भून लें। फिर इसमें टमाटर, दही और नमक डालकर दस मिनट तक पकायें। अब तले हुए आलू डालकर, मिश्रण में गरम पानी मिलाकर, हल्की आँच पर पाँच मिनट तक पकायें। दम आलू में काली मिर्च और गरम मसाला डालकर कुछ देर और पकायें। गरमागरम नान या रोटी के साथ परोसें।

कुछ टिप्स
दम आलू बनाने के लिए छोटे आलुओं का प्रयोग करें।

कड़ाही पनीर

कड़ाही पनीर को उसके नाम के अनुसार कड़ाही से ही परोसना चाहिए।

कड़ाही पनीर

सामग्री

250 ग्राम ताजा पनीर

3 शिमला मिर्च

4 प्याज

अदरक का एक टुकड़ा

1 चम्मच लाल मिर्च

2 तेज पत्ते

4 लौंग

1 टुकड़ा दालचीनी

4 चम्मच मक्खन

विधि

पनीर और शिमला मिर्च के लम्बे टुकड़े काट लें। प्याज, टमाटर, अदरक, नमक, मिर्च को मिलाकर पेस्ट बना लें। लौंग और दालचीनी को पीस लें। एक बर्तन में मक्खन डालकर गरम करें। इसमें तेज पत्ता, लौंग और दालचीनी को डालें। अब प्याज, टमाटर और लहसुन का पेस्ट डालें। इस मिश्रण को हल्की आँचपर तब तक भूनें, जब तक मसाला घी न छोड़ दें। अब पनीर और शिमला मिर्च के टुकड़े इस मिश्रण में मिलायें। हल्की आँचपर तब तक पकायें, जब तक शिमला मिर्च गल न जाये। आँच से उतार कर गरमागरम परोसें।

कुछ टिप्स

कड़ाही पनीर को बार-बार गरम न करें वर्ना पनीर का स्वाद बदल जायेगा और वह कड़ा हो जायेगा।

मलाई कोफ्ता

मलाई कोफ्ते केवल मलाई के बने नहीं होते हैं, परन्तु वे मलाई जितने नरम अवश्य होते हैं।

मलाई कोफ्ता

सामग्री

½ किलो आलू

2 चम्मच पनीर

2 चम्मच खोया

2 चम्मच मलाई

4-5 कटे हुए काजू

1 चम्मच किशमिश

2-3 बारीक कटी हुई हरी मिर्च

¼ चम्मच चीनी

1 चम्मच चीनी

1 चम्मच जीरा

1 चम्मच धनिया

1 चम्मच लाल मिर्च

½ चम्मच दालचीनी पाउडर

नमक (स्वादानुसार)

3 चम्मच तेल/घी कोफ्ते तलने के लिए

विधि

आलू उबाल लें। उन्हें छीलकर मथ लें और नमक मिला कर एक ओर रख दें। कोफ्ता बनाने के लिए बाकी सब मसाले, मेवा आदि एक साथ मिला लें।

आलू की पिट्ठी की गोल-गोल लोइयाँ बना लें। हर लोई के बीच में मसाले वाला मिश्रण भर लें और लोई वापस बन्द करके कोफ्ते बना लें। हर कोफ्ते को तेल में सुनहरा होने तक तल लें।

एक बर्तन में तेल गरम करें। उसमें प्याज, अदरक, लहसुन, खसखस डालकर भून लें। जब मसाला तेल छोड़ने लगे, तो उसमें टमाटर और मसाला पाउडर डाल दें। अब थोड़ी-सी चीनी और पिसी हुई मूँगफली मिलायें। धीरे-धीरे तरी गाढ़ी कर सकते हैं। यदि जरूरत हो, तो थोड़ा पानी मिलायें। एक उबाल देकर इस तरी में कोफ्ते डाल लें। गरमागरम नान के साथ मलाई कोफ्ता परोसें।

कुछ टिप्स

मलाई कोफ्ते बेहद नरम होते हैं, उन्हें भोजन से जरा पहले तरी में डालें और तुरन्त परोस दें वर्ना वे घुल कर व्यंजन का मजा खराब कर देंगे।

चिकन करी

चिकन से बनी यह डिश लाजवाब होती है। इसमें चिकन के स्थान पर मटन डाल कर मटन करी बना सकते हैं।

सामग्री

1 मध्यम साइज की मुर्गी
200 ग्राम प्याज
150 ग्राम टमाटर
100 ग्राम दही
अदरक, लहसुन, नमक,
धनिया, मिर्च, हल्दी,
मसाला, घी (अन्दाज से)

चिकन करी

विधि

मुर्गी के टुकड़े करके धो लीजिए। कुकर में घी गरम कर पिसा हुआ प्याज भूनिए। अदरक, लहसुन का पेस्ट, टमाटर व दही डालिए और घी अलग छोड़ने तक भूनिए। अब हल्दी, मिर्च, धनिया, मुर्गी के टुकड़े डालिए। हल्का लाल होने तक भूनिए। नमक व पानी अन्दाज से छोड़कर कुकर बन्द कीजिए। प्रेशर आने के बाद सात-आठ मिनट पकाइए। कुकर उतारकर ठण्डा होने दीजिए। फिर खोलकर परोसिए। गरम मसाला और कतरा हुआ हरा धनिया ऊपर से छिड़किए।

कुछ टिप्स

चिकन करी में चिकन मसाला डालने से खुशबू और स्वाद दोनों ही बढ़ जाते हैं।

New Modern

कीमा-कोफ्ता करी

यह माँसाहारी डिश अत्यन्त जायकेदार होती है।

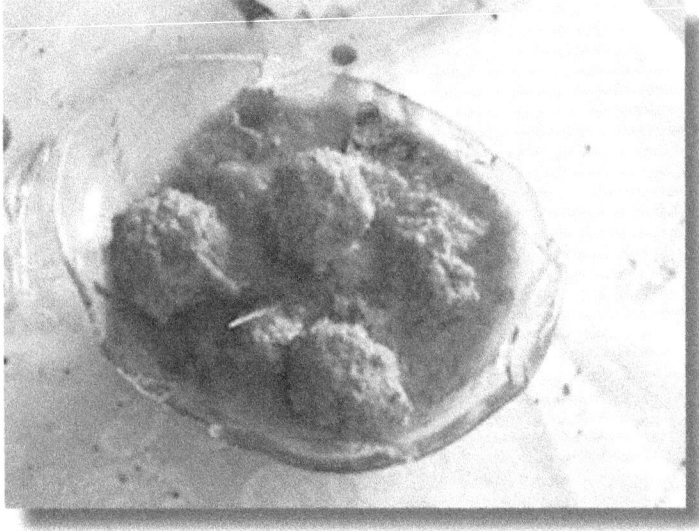

कीमा-कोफ्ता करी

सामग्री

250 ग्राम कीमा

2 मध्यम आकार के आलू

2 बड़े टमाटर

¼ भाग नारियल

1 नींबू

3 मध्यम आकार के प्याज

1½ इंच टुकड़ा अदरक का

4 कलियाँ लहसुन की

½ चम्मच खसखस

1½ चम्मच पिसा हुआ धनिया

4 लौंग

1 टुकड़ा दालचीनी

2 बड़े टमाटर

2 लाल सूखी मिर्च

1 हरी मिर्च

विधि

आलू उबाल, छीलकर कुचलिए। कोफ्ते बनाने के लिए कीमा, नारियल, खसखस साथ भूनिए और कूटिए। कुचले हुए आलू व नींबू मिलाकर गोलियाँ बनाइए। कड़ाही में घी डालकर कोफ्ते तल लीजिए। अब कुकर में घी डालकर कतरा हुआ प्याज भूनिए। पानी गरम होने पर नमक व कोफ्ते डालकर कुकर बन्द कर दीजिए। प्रेशर आने के बाद आँच मन्दी करके दो मिनट पकाइए। फिर कुकर ठण्डा होने दीजिए। प्लेट में शोरबे सहित निकालकर गरम मसाला, कतरा हुआ हरा धनिया छिड़किए। चावल या चपाती (रोटी) दोनों के साथ परोस सकती हैं।

कुछ टिप्स

कीमे के कोफ्ते बनाने के लिए कीमे के साथ उबले आलू के स्थान पर पिसी हुई चने की दाल का पेस्ट भी प्रयोग कर सकती हैं।

गोआनी लिवर करी

यह गोआ की मशहूर डिश है। जिसमें नारियल और सिरके का अनोखा मिश्रण है।

गोआनी लिवर करी

सामग्री

300 ग्राम कलेजी

½ भाग ताजा नारियल

1 चम्मच सौंफ

3 इलायची

1 टहनी मीठी नीम

1 बड़ा चम्मच सिरका

¼ चम्मच मेथी पाउडर

4 लाल मिर्च

2 मध्यम आकार का प्याज

5 कलियाँ लहसुन की

1 इंच टुकड़ा अदरक का

हल्दी, नमक व घी (अन्दाज से)

विधि

सौंफ कूट लीजिए। नारियल कद्दूकस कीजिए। लाल मिर्चों को थोड़े पानी में पकाकर पीस लीजिए। प्याज कतरिए। अदरक-लहसुन पीसिए।

कुकर में नमक और पानी के साथ कलेजी डालिए। तेज आँच पर प्रेशर आ जाये, तो आँच धीमी कर आठ मिनट पकाइए। कुकर को भाप निकालकर जल्दी खोलिए। एक पतीली में घी गरम कर प्याज भूनिए। मीठी नीम की पत्ती व अदरक-लहसुन की पेस्ट डालिए। लाल मिर्च, हल्दी, मेथी पाउडर, कुटी सौंफ मिलाइए। पानी से निकालकर कलेजी भी छोड़ दीजिए व भूनिए। लाल हो जाने पर 'स्टाक' (कलेजी का पानी) डाल दीजिए। सिरका छोड़िए, धीमी आँच पर पाँच मिनट पकाइए। उतारकर प्लेट में कतरे हुए धनिए व गरम मसाले के साथ सजाइए। सलाद के साथ परोसिए।

कुछ टिप्स

इस व्यंजन को अधिक मसालेदार बनाने के लिए कलेजी को भूनकर सब्जी में मिलायें।

चिकन मक्खनी

इस डिश को शाकाहारी मेहमानों के लिए भी बना सकते हैं, बस चिकन के स्थान पर पनीर के टुकड़े तरी में डाल दें।

चिकन मक्खनी

सामग्री

150 मि.ली. दही
50 ग्राम पिसे हुए बादाम
1½ चम्मच मिर्च पाउडर
¼ चम्मच पिसा हुआ तेजपत्ता
¼ चम्मच पिसी हुई दालचीनी
1 चम्मच पिसा हुआ गरम मसाला
4 छोटी इलायची
1 चम्मच अदरक का पेस्ट
1 चम्मच लहसुन का पेस्ट
400 ग्राम टमाटर
नमक (स्वादानुसार)
1 किलो मुर्गे का गोश्त (बिना हड्डी का)
75 ग्राम मक्खन
1 चम्मच तेल
2 कटे हुए प्याज
2 चम्मच कटा हुआ हरा धनिया
4 चम्मच ताजी क्रीम

विधि

दही, पिसे हुए बादाम, सूखे मसाले, अदरक, लहसुन, टमाटर और नमक एक कटोरे में अच्छी तरह मिलाकर पेस्ट बना लें।

एक बड़े बर्तन में गोश्त के टुकड़े रखकर ऊपर से यह पेस्ट डालकर एक तरफ रख दें। कड़ाही में मक्खन और तेल एक साथ गरम करें। उसमें कटे प्याज डालकर 3 मिनट तक भूनें। इसमें गोश्त का मिश्रण डालकर 7 से 10 मिनट तक भूनें। गोश्त पकने के बाद आँच से उतार लें। कुछ कटा हुआ हरा धनिया और क्रीम पके हुए गोश्त में मिलायें और एक उबाल दें। परोसने से पहले बाकी के कटे हरे धनिये से सजायें।

कुछ टिप्स

यदि ताजी क्रीम न मिले, तो दूध की ताजी मलाई फेंट कर भी डाल सकती हैं।

सादी नान पर घी लगाकर मक्खनी नान परोसी जा सकती है अन्यथा सादी नान भी अच्छी लगती है।

नान

सामग्री

4 कप मैदा
½ चम्मच बेकिंग पाउडर
1 चम्मच नमक
½ कप दूध
1 चम्मच चीनी
1 चम्मच तेल
1 चम्मच कलौंजी

विधि

आटा, नमक और बेकिंग पाउडर एक साथ छान लें और उसके बीच में गड्डा कर लें। उस गड्डे में चीनी, दूध और तेल मिलाकर डालें। आवश्यकतानुसार पानी डालते हुए नरम आटा मल लें। उसे गीले कपड़े से ढककर 15 मिनट के लिए रख दें। एक बार फिर गूँथकर आटे को 2-3 घण्टे के लिए छोड़ दें। तन्दूर या ओवन गरम कर लें। आटे की 8 बराबर लोइयाँ बना लें और 3-4 मिनट के लिए रख दें। ओवन में कुछ कलौंजी के दाने डाल कर छोड़ दें। हर लोई को हाथ से थपक कर लम्बा करें और ओवन में सेंक लें। सुनहरी, करारी नान को गरमागरम परोसें।

कुछ टिप्स

यदि आप अण्डा खाते हों, तो नान के आटे में दूध और तेल के साथ अण्डा भी डाल सकते हैं। इससे नान और फूली हुई बनेगी।

मिस्सी रोटी

मिस्सी रोटी तवे के अलावा ओवन या तन्दूर में भी बना सकते हैं।

मिस्सी रोटी

सामग्री

2 कप गेहूँ का आटा

2 कप बेसन

1 चम्मच जीरा

2 चम्मच कसूरी मेथी

नमक और लाल मिर्च

(स्वादानुसार)

चुटकी भर हल्दी पाउडर

2 चम्मच तेल

आटा गूँथने के लिए पानी

विधि

आटा, बेसन, नमक, मिर्च पाउडर, हल्दी पाउडर को एक साथ मिला लें। इस मिश्रण में कसूरी मेथी डालें और थोड़ा तेल भी मिलायें। धीरे-धीरे पानी मिलाते हुए नरम आटा गूँथ लें और उसे गीले कपड़े से ढककर 30 मिनट के लिए रख दें। रोटी बनाने से पहले आटे को एक बार फिर लोच देकर गूँथ लें और थोड़ी मोटी रोटी बेल लें। हर रोटी को तवे पर सेंककर घी लगाकर परोसें। आप चाहे तो बिना घी के भी मिस्सी रोटी परोस सकती हैं।

कुछ टिप्स

मिस्सी रोटी के आटे से मिस्सी परांठा भी बनाया
जा सकता है।

रूमाली रोटी

रूमाल के जैसी पतली और तह की गयी रोटियों को रूमाली रोटी कहते हैं।

रूमाली रोटी

सामग्री

1½ कप आटा
50 ग्राम मैदा
½ चम्मच बेकिंग पाउडर
2 चम्मच तेल
नमक (स्वादानुसार)
आटा गूँथने के लिए पानी

विधि

आटा, मैदा, नमक और बेकिंग पाउडर मिलाकर एक साथ छान लें। इस मिश्रण में तेल मिलायें और धीरे-धीरे पानी डालते हुए नरम आटा गूँथ लें। इस आटे को आधे घण्टे के लिए एक ओर रख दें। आटे को छोटी लोइयाँ तोड़कर, सूखा आटा लगाकर, पतली रोटी बेल लें। एक तवा लें। उसे उल्टा करके चूल्हे पर रख दें। उस पर रूमाली रोटी सेक लें। सिंकी हुई रोटी को रूमाल की तरह लपेट कर परोसें।

कुछ टिप्स

रूमाली रोटी बनाने के लिए काफी मेहनत और लगन की आवश्यकता होती है। इसलिए हिम्मत मत हारिए। याद रखिए, मेहनत ही सफलता की कुंजी है।

लच्छा परांठा

लच्छे परांठे का जायका तब है, जब वह इतना नरम हो कि दो उँगली से तोड़ा जा सकें।

लच्छा परांठा

सामग्री

2 कप आटा
50 ग्राम मैदा
1 चम्मच तेल
नमक (स्वादानुसार)
देशी घी/मक्खन
आटा गूँथने के लिए पानी

विधि

आटा, मैदा, नमक और तेल डालकर आटा गूँथ लें। आधे घण्टे के लिए उसे गीले कपड़े से ढककर रख दें। एक लोई लेकर थोड़ी-सी बेल लें। उसके ऊपर पिघला हुआ घी लगा दें। चाकू से लम्बाई में काटकर भीतर की ओर मोड़ दें। हर मोड़ पर घी लगाते जायें। परांठे की तरह बेल लें। गरम तवे पर डालकर घी/मक्खन में अच्छी तरह सेंक लें। हल्की आँच पर दोनों ओर से सुनहरा होने तक सेंकें और गरमागरम परोसें।

कुछ टिप्स

आटा गूँथते समय थोड़ी-सी मलाई और दो चम्मच दूध मिलाने से परांठे नरम बनते हैं।

पुलाव

बासमती चावल, सब्जियों और मेवे से बनी यह बिरयानी न केवल स्वादिष्ट होती है, बल्कि पौष्टिक भी होती है।

पुलाव

सामग्री

2 कप बासमती चावल

1 कप मिली-जुली सब्जियाँ (गोभी, आलू, गाजर, बीन आदि)

150 ग्राम हरी मटर

3 कटे हुए प्याज

2 बारीक कटी हुई हरी मिर्च

नमक स्वादानुसार

1 चम्मच लाल मिर्च पाउडर

2 चम्मच दालचीनी पाउडर

½ चम्मच जीरा

½ चम्मच काली मिर्च पाउडर

4 टमाटर

½ कप दही

4 चम्मच तेल या घी

½ चम्मच सरसों

3 चम्मच मेवा (काजू और किशमिश)

विधि

बनाने से पूर्व बासमती चावल अच्छी तरह धो कर एक घण्टे के लिए भिगो दें। फिर एक बर्तन में भीगे चावल, दो कप पानी और थोड़े से नमक और मेवा के साथ पका लें। सभी सब्जियों को काटकर अलग-अलग भून लें। एक चम्मच तेल बर्तन में डालें। उसमें सरसों, हरी मिर्च, दालचीनी और जीरा पाउडर, लौंग, काली मिर्च पाउडर डालकर आधा मिनट तक भून लें। फिर उसमें कटा हुआ प्याज डाल कर गुलाबी होने तक भून लें। इसमें नमक और लाल मिर्च पाउडर डालें और चलायें। अब इसमें बारीक कटे हुए टमाटर डालकर भून लें। दही को मथकर इस मिश्रण में मिलाकर 10 सेकेण्ड तक पकायें। सभी भुनी हुई सब्जियाँ चावलों में डालकर हल्के हाथ से मिलायें ताकि चावल के दाने टूटें नहीं। अब इसे तीन-चार मिनट तक पकायें। इस पुलाव को एक बड़ी तशतरी में पलटकर परोसें। कटे हुए मेवा और हरे धनिये से सजायें।

कुछ टिप्स

पुलाव के साथ बूँदी का रायता और हरे ध निये-पुदीने की चटनी बेहद स्वादिष्ट लगती है।

मुगलई बिरियानी

इस बिरयानी का जायका और खुशबू आपको मुगलकाल में पहुँचा देगा।

मुगलई बिरियानी

सामग्री

500 ग्राम बासमती चावल

500 ग्राम गोश्त (चिकन या मटन)

125 ग्राम प्याज

200 ग्राम दही

100 मि.ली. दूध

1 नींबू

50 दाने बादाम

4 लाल मिर्च

10 पुदीना पत्ता

5 हरी मिर्च

4 आलू

घी, जीरा, नमक, अदरक, लहसुन, हरा धनिया, थोड़ा-सा केसर (अन्दाज से)

विधि

गोश्त को साफकर धो लीजिए। प्याज कतर लीजिए। धनिया व पुदीने के पत्ते कतरिए। अदरक, लहसुन, हरी और लाल मिर्च पीसिए। मसाले और दही को गोश्त में मिलाकर डेढ़ घण्टे तक रख दीजिए। कुकर में घी डालकर प्याज लाल कीजिए। प्याज निकालकर मसाला और गोश्त कुकर में छोड़िए। भूनकर नमक और एक कप पानी डालिए। कुकर बन्दकर प्रेशर आने के बाद दस मिनट तक पकाइए। भाप निकालकर कुकर को जल्दी खोलिए फिर मसाला-गोश्त निकाल लीजिए। कुकर में चावल और 3½ कप पानी डालिए। बन्दकर प्रेशर आने के बाद दो मिनट पकाइए। दो मिनट बाद भाप निकालकर कुकर जल्दी खोलिए। चावल निकालकर कुकर में घी डालिए। पिसी हुई लौंग इलायची, जीरा, धनिया, पुदीना, बादाम और नमक छोड़िए। चावलों को सावधानी से इस मसाले में मिलाइए। नींबू निचोड़कर अच्छी तरह उलट-पुलट कर मिला दीजिए। केशर को दूध में घोलकर आधे चावलों में मिलाइए। अब बड़ी देगची में चावल, गोश्त की तह बारी-बारी से लगाइए। हर तह पर कुछ तले प्याज के लच्छे रखती जाइए। बचा हुआ दूध और कुछ घी ऊपर से ही छोड़िए। अब देगची को बन्दकर चावलों को दम दीजिए। निकालकर आलू की तली चकलियों या तले लच्छों से सजाकर गरम-गरम परोसिए। यह मुगलई बिरियानी सभी सामिष पार्टियों में पसन्द किया जाने वाला एक बहुत लोकप्रिय व्यंजन है।

कुछ टिप्स

मुगलई बिरयानी को रायते और प्याज के लच्छे के साथ परोसें।

अण्डे-टमाटर वाले चावल

मेहमानों के लिए अण्डे, टमाटर से सजी यह पुलाव-प्लेट एक 'स्पेशल' डिश होगी।

अण्डे–टमाटर वाले चावल

सामग्री

1½ कप बासमती चावल

6 अण्डे

3 समान आकार वाले टमाटर

1 चम्मच चीनी

½ कप किसा हुआ पनीर

½ कप टमाटर सॉस

2 बड़े प्याज

1 बड़ा आलू

हरा धनिया, हरी मिर्च,

नमक, घी (अन्दाज से)

विधि

देगची में घी छोड़कर कतरे हुए प्याज भूनिए। चावल धोकर डालिए। नमक डालकर इतना पानी छोड़िए कि चावल जरा कच्चे रहें और पानी सूख जाये। अब चावलों के दो भाग करके कुकर के दो सेपरेटर्स में डालिए। टमाटरों को आधा-आधा काटकर मध्य से खोखला कीजिए। सेपरेटर में जमे चावलों पर हाथ से तीन छेद बनाइए व टमाटरों की ये तीन कटोरियाँ इन गड्ढों में भर दीजिए। अब टमाटर के खोल में एक अण्डा तोड़कर बिना फेंटे डाल दीजिए। पीला भाग टमाटर के खोल के भीतर रहे, सफेद भाग आसपास कुछ बिखर सकता है। अब इन अण्डों के ऊपर किसा हुआ पनीर, कतरी हुई हरी मिर्च, हरा धनिया व नमक मिलाकर बुरकिए। फिर चित्र के अनुसार तीन अण्डों के मध्य भाग को केन्द्र बनाते हुए चावलों में गहरी विभाजन-रेखा खींचिए और इन रेखाओं में टमाटर सॉस भर दीजिए। दूसरा सेपरेटर भी इसी तरह टमाटर के तीन खोल व तीन अण्डों के साथ तैयार कर लीजिए।

कुकर में थोड़ा पानी डालकर ग्रिड (जाली) रखिए व उसपर दोनों सेपरेटर्स जमाकर कुकर बन्द कर दीजिए। फिर प्रेशर आते ही कुकर उतार लीजिए व ठण्डा होने तक चावलों को भाप में पकने दीजिए। इसके बाद सावधानी से चावलों के गोल जमे थक्के निकालकर सीधे-सीधे दो प्लेटों में रखिए। ऊपर से आलू के तले लच्छे सजा लीजिए। प्लेट में चावलों के आसपास भी कतरे हरे धनिये से एक रेखा खींचिए।

स्पेनिश राइस

यह स्पेनिश पुलाव बड़ा स्वादिष्ट होगा और देखने में भी सुन्दर लगेगा।

स्पेनिश राइस

सामग्री

2 कप बासमती चावल
2 बड़े चम्मच चीनी
200 ग्राम शिमला मिर्च
1 कप उबली हुई स्पाघेट्टी या मैक्रोनी
½ कप टमाटर सॉस
2 मध्यम प्याज
पनीर, लहसुन, अदरक, गरम
मसाला, नमक, घी (अन्दाज से)

विधि

कुकर में घी डालकर पहले चीनी इतना भूनिए कि वह ब्राउन रंग की हो जाये। इससे सारे चावलों में रंग आ जायेगा। अब प्याज, लहसुन, अदरक के पतले लच्छे डालकर भूनिए। फिर चावल धोकर डालिए। कुछ देर भूनकर नमक और पानी डालिए। पक जाने पर यह ब्राउन रंग का पुलाव होगा।

अलग घी में शिमला मिर्च या कैपसीकम के टुकड़े तलिए। जरा-सा नमक और टमाटर सॉस मिलाइए। कुकर में से चावल निकालिए (पहली बार जरा कच्चे ही रहने चाहिए, पूरे न गलें) एक तह चावलों की और एक तह टमाटर सॉस मिली व तली मिर्च की लगाइए। क्रमशः तीन-चार बार। फिर कुकर को बन्दकर चावलों को दम दीजिए।

प्लेट सज्जा: बड़ी 'राइस प्लेट' में चावल भरकर मध्य में एक गड्ढा बनाइए। उसमें उबली हुई स्पाघेट्टी या मैक्रोनी भरिए। अब आसपास टमाटर सॉस से रेखाओं में सज्जा कीजिए। इसे पनीर व कतरे हरे धनिये से भी सज्जा-नमूना बना सकती है।

कुछ टिप्स

अच्छे स्वाद के लिए इस पुलाव को आप
राइस-कुकर में भी पका सकती है।

दहीबड़ा

दहीबड़ा छोटे और बड़े सभी उम्र के लोगों को पसन्द आता है

दहीबड़ा

सामग्री

बड़े के लिए:

1 कप उड़द की दाल
नमक (स्वादानुसार)

तलने के लिए:

1 किलो गाढ़ा दही
½ कप कटा हुआ अदरक
बारीक कटा हुआ हरा धनिया
1-2 कटी हुई हरी मिर्च
नमक (स्वादानुसार)
2 चम्मच भुना हुआ जीरा पाउडर
लाल मिर्च (स्वादानुसार)

विधि

उड़द की दाल को साफ करके रातभर के लिए भिगो दें। सुबह दाल को पीस लें व नमक मिला लें। कड़ाही में तेल गरम करें। हाथ से फेंटकर पिसी हुई दाल के बड़े तल लें। गरम बड़ों को ठण्डे पानी में 20-30 मिनट के लिए भिगो दें। फिर हाथ से दबाकर सारा पानी निकाल दें और बड़े एक तरफ रख लें। दही फेंट लें। उसमें नमक, लाल मिर्च और भुना हुआ जीरा मिला दें। एक गहरे बर्तन में बड़े रख लें और उन पर दही डाल दें। ऊपर से थोड़ी हरी चटनी डालें और कटे हुए धनिया से सजायें। ठण्डे दहीबड़े परोसें ।

कुछ टिप्स

यदि आपको मीठे दहीबड़े अच्छे लगते हैं, तो परोसने से पूर्व दहीबड़ों पर इमली की मीठी सोंट डाल सकते हैं।

बथुये का रायता

बथुये का रायता सरदी के मौसम में शरीर को गरमाहट देता है, क्योंकि बथुये की तासीर गरम होती है।

बथुये का रायता

सामग्री

। कप दही
½ कप बथुआ (उबला, मथ हुआ)
। चम्मच भुना हुआ जीरा पाउडर
नमक और लाल मिर्च
(स्वादानुसार)

विधि

दही को मथ लें। उसमें बथुये का पेस्ट मिला दें। यदि बहुत गाढ़ा लगे, तो थोड़ा ठण्डा दूध मिला दें। नमक, जीरा पाउडर और मिर्च डालकर अच्छी तरह मिला लें। एक घण्टे के लिए फ्रिज में रखें, फिर परोसें। ठण्डा बथुये का रायता गरमागरम आलू के परांठों के साथ बहुत अच्छा लगता है।

कुछ टिप्स

थोड़े से उबले, मथ हुए बथुये को आटे में भरकर परांठे बनायें और गरमागरम परांठे का ठण्डे बथुये के रायते के साथ आनन्द उठायें।

फ्रूट रायता

फलों का रायता वजन कम करने वालों के लिए अच्छी डिश है।

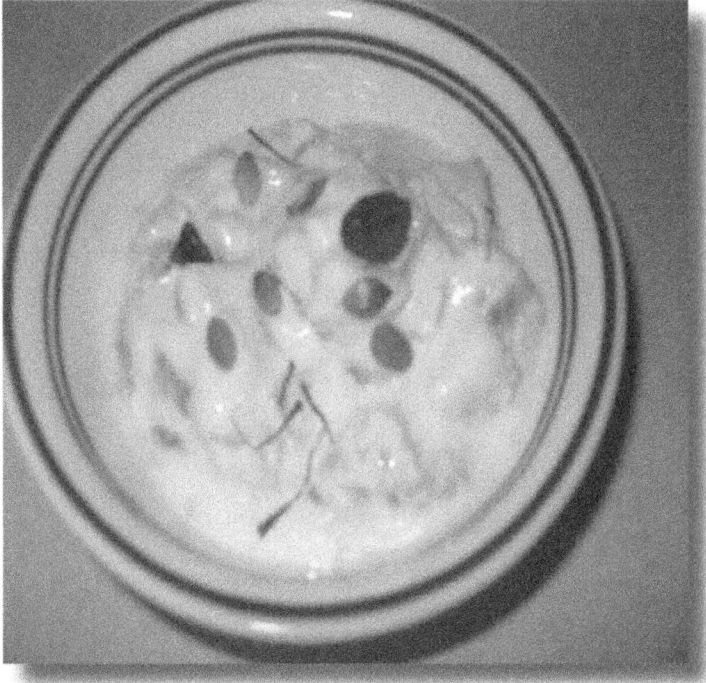

फ्रूट रायता

सामग्री

2 कप दही

3 केले

1 छोटा अनन्नास

2 सेब

1 पका हुआ आम

1 कप अनार के दाने

बारीक कटा हुआ हरा धनिया

नमक, चीनी,

काली मिर्च (स्वादानुसार)

विधि

दही को मथनी से मथ लें। उसमें नमक, काली मिर्च और चीनी मिला दें। यदि बहुत गाढ़ा लगे, तो उसे थोड़ा ठण्डा दूध या पानी मिलाकर पतला कर लें। सभी फल छोटे-छोटे टुकड़ों में काट लें और दही में मिला दें। फ्रूट रायता तैयार है। कटे हुए हरे धनिये और अनार के दानों से सजा कर ठण्डा परोसें।

कुछ टिप्स

इस रायते में आप अपनी पसन्द के कोई भी फल डाल सकती हैं।

सलाद ड्रेसिंग

यह ड्रेसिंग सादे सलाद को भी लुभावना बना देती है।

सामग्री

3 चम्मच कॉर्नफ्लार
1 कप दूध
नमक (स्वादानुसार)
1 चम्मच सिरका
¼ चम्मच कस्टर्ड

सलाद ड्रेसिंग

विधि

छोटे तीन चम्मच कार्नफ्लोर लेकर थोड़े पानी में घोलिए। एक कप दूध गरमकर उसमें मिलाइए। चलाते हुए तीन मिनट तक पकाइए। ठण्डी होने दीजिए। अब एक बड़ा चम्मच सिरका लेकर उसमें एक चाय का चम्मच भर चीनी, नमक और थोड़ी राई मिलाइए और यह मिश्रण दूध के बने कस्टर्ड में मिला लीजिए।

कुछ टिप्स

सलाद स्वादिष्ट होने के साथ-साथ पौष्टिक भी होता है।

फ्रेंच ड्रेसिंग

यह ड्रेसिंग से हर डिश में एक नया जायका आ जाता है।

फ्रेंच ड्रेसिंग

सामग्री

1 चम्मच नींबू का रस
3 चम्मच सलाद का तेल
2 चम्मच पिसा हुआ प्याज
1 चम्मच पिसा हुआ लहसुन
1 चम्मच पिसी हुई सरसों
1 चम्मच लाल मिर्च पाउडर
नमक, काली मिर्च (स्वादानुसार)

विधि

तीन चम्मच जैतून या सलाद का तेल और एक चम्मच नींबू का रस मिलायें। अब इसमें दो चम्मच पिसा हुआ प्याज, एक चम्मच पिसा हुआ लहसुन, एक चम्मच पिसी हुई राई, एक चम्मच लाल मिर्च या आधी चम्मच लाल व आधी चम्मच काली मिर्च और नमक मिलाइए। एक घण्टे तक ये मसाले भीगे रहें। फिर निकालकर प्रयोग में लाइए।

कुछ टिप्स

नींबू के रस की जगह तीन चम्मच सिरका भी मिला सकती हैं।

New Mode

गुलदस्ते के रूप में सलाद

फूलों के बुके तो आपने बहुत देखे होंगे, अब देखिए सलाद का बुके।

गुलदस्ते के रूप में सलाद

सामग्री

कुछ सलाद के पत्ते

1 पत्तागोभी

1 गाजर

2 उबले हुए आलू

1 चुकन्दर

2 टमाटर

100 ग्राम पनीर

1 मूली

कुछ धनिया और पुदीना पत्ती

1 नींबू

हरी मिर्च

काली मिर्च

नमक (स्वादानुसार)

विधि

एक गहरा प्लेट या बर्तन लें। अब उसे चारों ओर से लेट्यूस या बन्धगोभी के पत्तों से ढक लें। बीच में बन्धगोभी के पत्तों को छोटा-छोटा काट लें और साथ में उबले हुए आलू के टुकड़े, गाजर के छोटे टुकड़े, बीटरूट के टुकड़े, टमाटर के टुकड़े, पनीर के टुकड़े, कटे हुए पुदीना और धनिया पत्ता डालकर सलाद को आकर्षित एवं स्वादिष्ट बनायें। स्वाद के लिए हरी मिर्च, लाल मिर्च पाउडर, नमक और नींबू का रस आदि का प्रयोग करें।

कुछ टिप्स

गुलदस्ते के रुप में यह सलाद बड़ा ही पौष्टिक, स्वादिष्ट एवं आकर्षक होता है।

आपके व आपके परिवार के स्वास्थ्य और सौन्दर्य के लिए सलाद जरूरी है।

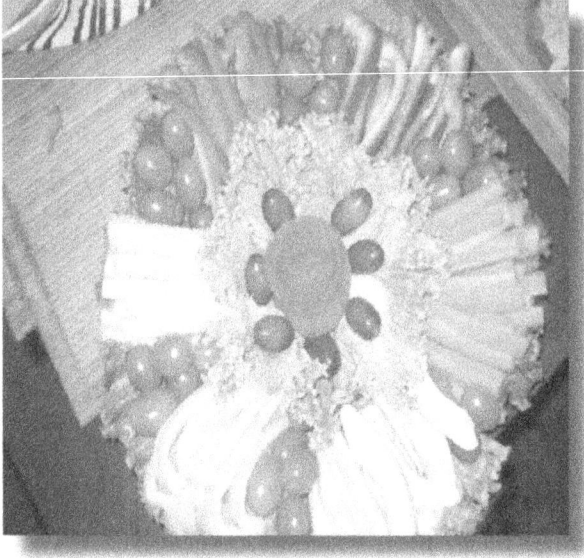

सलाद—सज्जा

सामग्री

सलाद के पत्ते

मूली के पत्ते

2–3 गाजर

1 मूली

1 प्याज

1 टमाटर

1 खीरा

½ कप उबली हुई मटर

कटा हुआ हरा धनिया

1 चम्मच नींबू का रस

नमक, काली मिर्च (स्वादानुसार)

विधि

पत्ती की आकृति की एक गहरे रंग की प्लेट लीजिए। प्रारम्भ में मूली की दो लम्बी कतलियों को कटे किनारे वाली चौड़ी पत्तियों के रूप में सजाइए। सलाद पत्ती को भी इस शक्ल में काटकर सजा सकती हैं। प्लेट के नुकीले सिरे पर मूली की पत्तियों या सलाद पत्तियों के साथ टमाटर का एक फूल सजा दीजिए। प्लेट के बीचों-बीच अम्बी की शक्ल में काटकर मूली की एक पत्ती रखिए। उसके चारों ओर उबले हुए मटर के दानों को दो जुड़ी रेखाओं के रूप में जोड़िए। उसके आसपास मूली, गाजर, खीरे (जो भी चीजें हों) के फूल काटकर सजा दीजिए अब प्लेट को उठाकर स्टैण्ड पर रखिए। सलाद पर मध्य भाग में कतरा हुआ हरा धनिया सजाइए। व आधा नींबू निचोड़ दीजिए। चाहें तो नमक, काली मिर्च भी बुरक लें। सलाद की एक सुन्दर प्लेट तैयार है।

ये मात्र चार सुझाव हैं। अपनी सूझ-बूझ से सलाद सजाने के आप कई और कलात्मक ढंग अपना सकती हैं। प्रयोग कीजिए और सलाद की उन्हीं सब्जियों को तरह-तरह से सजाकर आकर्षक ढंग से परोसिए ताकि जो कच्ची सब्जियाँ नहीं खाते, वे भी खाने की आदत डाल सके।

कुछ टिप्स

सलाद-सज्जा को केवल मेहमानों के लिए ही नहीं, अपने दैनिक भोजन की मेज के लिए भी अपनाना चाहिए।

मिठाई दिलबहार

दिलबहार एक सदाबहार मिठाई है।

मिठाई दिलबहार

सामग्री

250 ग्राम छेना
200 ग्राम खोआ
300 ग्राम चीनी
1 चम्मच सूजी
कतरे हुए मेवे
इलायची
1 बड़ा चम्मच घी

विधि

एक लीटर भैंस के दूध को नींबू से फाड़कर छेना तैयार करें। यह 250 ग्राम के लगभग निकल आयेगा। इसे भारी पत्थर के नीचे दबाकर पहले जमा लें। फिर मसलकर उसमें एक चम्मच सूजी मिलायें। 300 ग्राम चीनी में से 100 ग्राम अलग निकालकर पीसकर रख लें। शेष 200 ग्राम चीनी की एक तार की चाशनी बनायें। अब इसमें छेने की टिकिया बनाकर डाल दें और तक तक पकने दें, जब तक कि चीनी जमने के लायक गाढ़ी न हो जाये। इसके बाद टिकिया कड़ाही से निकालकर अलग-अलग फैला दें। ठण्डी होने पर ये सूख जायेंगी। तब इन्हें मध्य से काटकर दो भागों में कर लें।

कड़ाही में एक बड़ा चम्मच घी डालकर खोआ मन्दी आँच पर भूनें। कतरे हुए मेवे, इलायचीदाना मिलाकर उतारें व पिसी हुई 100 ग्राम चीनी मिलाकर चला दें।

अब छेने की टिकियों के दानों भाग उठायें, बीच में यह खोआ मिश्रण भरकर दोनों भागों को परस्पर दबा दें। मेहमानों के लिए एक नये ढंग की स्वादिष्ट व आकर्षक दिखने वाली मिठाई तैयार है।

कुछ टिप्स

दिल के आकार की यह मिठाई बिना दूध के मिश्रण वाले भरावन के भी स्वादिष्ट लगती है।

तिरंगी टिक्की

यह मिठाई खाने और देखने में अत्यन्त अनोखी है।

तिरंगी टिक्की

सामग्री

8 स्लाइस डबल रोटी
1 प्याला दूध
200 ग्राम दूध का छेना
250 ग्राम चीनी
कुछ दाने चैरी मुरब्बा के
घी तलने के लिए

विधि

डबल रोटी के किनारों का लाल भाग खुरचकर इन्हें गोल आकृति में मध्य से काट लें। एक थाली में दूध फैलायें। साथ ही कड़ाही में घी गरम करें। डबल रोटी का एक-एक टुकड़ा दूध में उलट-पुलट कर पूरा गलने से पहले निकाल लें व उसे कड़ाही में तेज आँच पर तल लें। अब इन तले हुए टुकड़ों को चाशनी में डालकर निकाल लें।

बची हुई चाशनी में दो चम्मच दूध डालकर फिर आँच पर चढ़ायें। मैल अलग हो जाने पर छान लें। फिर छेने की गोल-गोल टिकिया (डबल रोटी की गोल टिक्की से लगभग आधी) बनाकर इसे चाशनी में पका लें। चाशनी जमने लायक हो जाये, तो उतार कर टिकियों को तुरन्त डबल रोटी की तली हुई टुकड़ियों पर जमा दें। ठण्डी होने पर वे जम जायेंगी। इसलिए गरम रहते ही छेने की टिकियों के ऊपर एक-एक चैरी का दाना भी रख दें। टिकियों के ठण्डे होने पर तीनों भाग परस्पर जुड़ जायेंगे। अब इन्हें उठाकर प्लेट में सजा लें।

कुछ टिप्स

चैरी के मुरब्बे के स्थान पर डब्बाबन्द अनन्नास
का भी प्रयोग कर सकती हैं।

छेना मुरगी

केवल छेना की यह मिठाई बड़ी स्वादिष्ट होती है।

छेना मुरगी

सामग्री
2 लीटर दूध
500 ग्राम चीनी
कुटी हुई इलायची

विधि

भैंस का खालिस दूध लेकर उसे दो नींबू के रस से फाड़ लें। कपड़े में छानकर पानी निचोड़ें, फिर जमाकर भारी चपटे पत्थर से दबा लें। थाली-सी जम जाने पर चाक पर छोटी-छोटी टुकड़ियाँ काटें व कपड़े पर फैला दें ताकि पानी सूख जाये।

अब चीनी की एक तार की चाशनी पकायें। उसमें सभी टुकड़ियाँ और कुटी हुई इलायची डाल दें। पहले मध्यम व फिर मन्दी आँच पर, तब तक पकने दें, जब तक कि चाशनी फिर जमने लायक न हो जाये। उसके बाद उतारकर चलाती रहिए ताकि छेने की मिठाइयाँ या छेना मुरगी का एक-एक दाना सूखकर अलग-अलग हो जाये। केवल छेने की यह मिठाई बड़ी स्वादिष्ट होती है। इसे गहरे रंग की सुन्दर-सी प्लेट में सजाकर परोसें।

कुछ टिप्स
घर मे पनीर न बनाना चाहें तो बाजार से भी पनीर खरीद सकती हैं।

कोकोनट बरफी

नारियल का अनोखा स्वाद और खुशबू किसी भी डिश का स्वाद बढ़ा देते हैं। नारियल पसन्द करने वालों के लिए यह खास मिठाई है।

कोकोनट बरफी

सामग्री

1 मध्यम आकार का कच्चा नारियल
½ किलो खोआ
1 किलो चीनी
1 बड़ी चम्मच घी

विधि

नारियल को छीलकर कद्दूकस कर लें। खोये को एक अलग कड़ाही में डालकर मन्दी आँच पर थोड़े घी में भून लें। लाल न होने पाये।

दूसरी कड़ाही में चीनी की चाशनी चढ़ा दें। एक तार निकलने पर इसमें किसा हुआ नारियल छोड़ दें और पकायें। जब चाशनी फिर गाढ़ी होकर तीन तार छोड़ने लगे यानी जमने लायक हो जाये, तब खोआ डालकर उतार लें और खूब चलायें। फिर एक थाली में घी चुपड़ कर मिश्रण उसमें पलटें व जमा दें। ठण्डी होकर बरफी जम जायेगी। चाकू से इसकी टुकड़ियाँ काट लें। इसे भी गहरे रंग की प्लेट में सजाना चाहिए। साथ में गुलाब की पत्तियाँ सजा सकती हैं।

हाँ, कच्चा नारियल न होने पर आप सूखा नारियल किस करके प्रयोग में ला सकती हैं। उसे चाशनी में पकाने की जरूरत नहीं रहेगी। खोये के साथ सीधा गाढ़ी चाशनी में मिलाकर जमा सकती हैं।

कुछ टिप्स

इस बरफी को व्रत में भी खा सकते हैं।

रस बड़ा

'रसबड़ा' गुलाबजामुन या रसगुल्ले से अलग प्रकार की मिठाई होती है।

रस बड़ा

सामग्री

250 ग्राम उड़द की दाल
500 ग्राम खोआ
500 ग्राम चीनी
कतरे हुए मेवे
तलने के लिए घी

विधि

उड़द की दाल को पीसकर आटा बना लीजिए या रात को भिगोकर सुबह पीसकर पीठी बना लीजिए। पीठी, मेवे और खोआ को मिलाकर गोल-गोल बड़े बनाकर बीच में छेद कीजिए और कड़ाही में घी गरम करके तल लीजिए। आँच मन्दी रखनी चाहिए कि बड़े ठीक से सिक जायें।

अब चीनी की एक तार की चाशनी बनाइए और गरम-गरम बड़े उसमें छोड़ती जाइए। बड़ों के मध्य जो छेद हैं, उनमें एक-एक काजू भर कर प्लेट में सजाइए। चाहें तो प्लेट के बीच अतिरिक्त काजू भी सजा सकती हैं।

कुछ टिप्स
सजाने के लिए काजू के साथ बादाम और पिस्ता भी डाल सकती हैं।

मूँग की बरफी

धुली हुई मूँग की दाल से बनी बरफी पीले रंग की होती है और साबुत मूँग से बनी बरफी हरे रंग की होती है।

मूँग की बरफी

सामग्री

250 ग्राम साबुत मूँग

250 ग्राम खोआ

250 ग्राम घी

500 ग्राम पिसी हुई चीनी

कतरे हुए मेवे

इलायची दाना

विधि

मूँग को साफ करके दरदरा आटा पिसा लीजिए। कड़ाही में घी डालकर यह आटा मन्दी आँच पर भूनिए। जब घी अलग छोड़ने लगे, तो खोआ डालकर पाँच मिनट और भूनिए। उतारकर कतरे मेवे, इलायची दाना और पिसी हुई चीनी मिलाइए और थाली में जमा दीजिए। जम जाने पर टुकड़ियों को काटकर प्लेट में सजाइए।

कुछ टिप्स

इस तरह की हरे रंग की बरफी पिस्ते की भी बनायी जाती है। पर आजकल पिस्ता अधिक महँगा होने से आप पिस्ते के दाने इस बरफी के ऊपर ही सजा सकती हैं। धुली हुई दाल के आटे की बरफी बनायें, तो मीठा हरा रंग इस्तेमाल किया जा सकता है। लेकिन रंग डालने की बजाय छिलके वाली दाल का प्राकृतिक रंग ही आप रखें, तो अच्छा रहेगा।

शाही टोस्ट

शाही टोस्ट अत्यन्त आसानी से बनायी जाने वाली मिठाई है।

शाही टोस्ट

सामग्री

8 डबल रोटी के बड़े स्लाइस
6 चम्मच चीनी
½ लीटर दूध
1 टुकड़ा नारियल
8 दाने चैरी मुरब्बा
चुटकी भर पीला रंग
तलने के लिए घी

विधि

तेज छुरी से डबलरोटी के सात टुकड़ों को बरफी की टुकड़ी की तरह लम्बी आकृति में काटिए। इन्हें कड़ाही में घी डालकर तलिए व गुलाबी होने से पहले निकाल लीजिए। आठवाँ टुकड़ा किसी शीशी के ढक्कन से गोल काटिए। इसे भी तल लीजिए।

दूध को कड़ाही में औटांकर रबड़ी बनाइए। चीनी मिलाकर किसा हुआ नारियल मिलाइए व उतार लीजिए। एक बड़ी प्लेट में सात बड़े स्लाइस चित्र में दिखाये अनुसार एक सितारे की शक्ल में जमाइए, मध्य में गोल टुकड़ा रखकर आकृति बराबर कर लीजिए। अब सातों स्लाइसों के ऊपर किनारों पर दो-दो सेण्टीमीटर स्थान छोड़कर रबड़ी फैलाइए। उसी आकृति में अब दो छोटी चम्मच भर चीनी, दो चम्मच पानी और पीला मीठा रंग मिलाकर पकाइए। उतारकर एक डण्डी की मदद से सफेद रबड़ी के चारों ओर यह पीली धारी बनाइए। फिर हर टोस्ट के ऊपर मध्य भाग में एक चैरी का दाना सजा दीजिए।

कुछ टिप्स

प्लेट के खाली भागों में हरे कागज की कटावदार पत्तियाँ सजाकर आप इस खूबसूरत प्लेट को और खूबसूरत बना सकती हैं। मेहमान देखते ही रह जायेंगे।

गाजर का हलवा

जाड़े के मौसम में गाजर बहुतायात से उपलब्ध होती है। यह काफी सस्ती भी होती है, जबकि पौष्टिकता में यह सबसे अधिक गुणकारी है। दूध के साथ मिलकर गाजर की पौष्टिकता और भी बढ़ जाती है और स्वादिष्ट नाश्ता सभी पसन्द भी करते हैं।

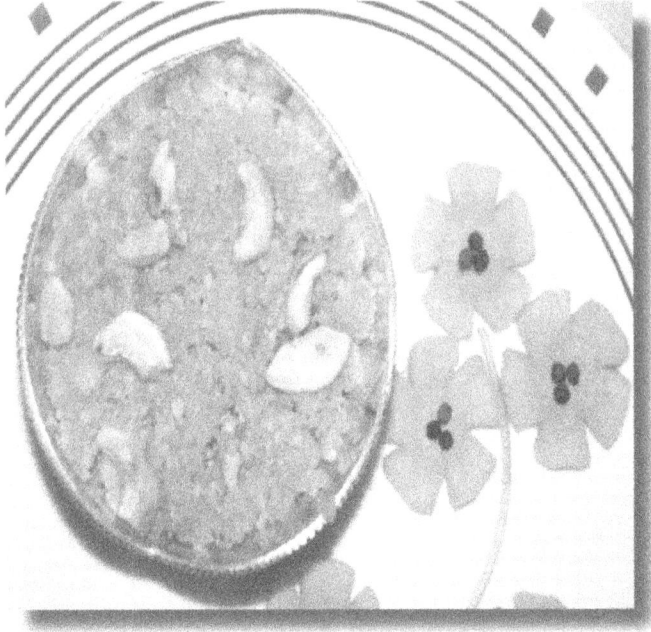

गाजर का हलवा

सामग्री

। किलो गाजर

। लीटर दूध

2 चम्मच घी/मक्खन

चीनी (स्वादानुसार)

। कप किशमिश, काजू, बादाम

विधि

एक किलो गाजर लेकर उनके रोयें आदि साफ करके पहले अच्छी तरह धो लें। फिर उन्हें कद्दूकस में कस लें। एक लीटर दूध में डालकर आग पर चढ़ायें। पहले तेज आँच पर चार-पाँच उबाल आने दें, फिर मध्यम आँच पर पकने दें। अन्त में चीनी डालकर मन्दी आँच पर पकायें। घी या मक्खन इच्छानुसार डाल सकती हैं। पानी और दूध सूख जाने पर थोड़ी देर मन्दी आँच पर भूनें, फिर प्लेट में निकाल कर किशमिश और बादाम की गिरियों से या चित्र के अनुसार किशमिश और काजू से सजायें। सज्जा में फूलों, बेलों के छिजाइन इस स्वादिष्ट प्लेट का आकर्षण और बढ़ा देंगे। इस ट्रे नुमा लम्बी प्लेट के साथ फिर मनी-प्लाण्ट की बेल भी जरा सजाकर देखिए तो!

कुछ टिप्स

गाजर विटामिन 'ए' का मुख्य स्रोत है।

सूजी का हलवा

नाश्ते के लिए जल्दी बनने वाला यह एक मीठा पौष्टिक व्यंजन है।

सूजी का हलवा

सामग्री

1 कप सूजी
2 चम्मच घी
2 कप चीनी
कुछ इलायची के बीज
कुछ किशमिश

विधि

पहले चीनी में पानी मिलाकर गरम कीजिए। एक उबाल आने पर चाशनी को छानकर समीप रख लीजिए। अब कड़ाही में इतना घी डालिए कि सूजी डूब भर सके। सूजी को मन्दी आँच में गुलाबी होने तक भूनिए। जब घी अलग होने लगे, तो आँच धीमी करके चाशनी छोड़िए और फिर एकदम आँच तेज करके हलवे को जल्दी-जल्दी चलाइए। इलायची दाने और किशमिश बनते समय ही छोड़िए ताकि किशमिश फूल जाये और इलायची से हलवा सुगन्धित हो जाये। चाहें तो केसर डाल कर केसरिया भी बना सकती हैं।

हलवे को अब प्लेटों में डालकर ऊपर से कतरे मेवों से सजाइए। नाश्ते के लिए जल्दी बनने वाला यह एक मीठा पौष्टिक व्यंजन है।

कुछ टिप्स

सूजी की जगह मूँग की दाल का आटा भून कर दाल का हलवा भी इसी तरह बना सकती हैं। पर भीगी दाल की ताजी पिसी पीठी भून कर बनाया गया दाल का हलवा अधिक स्वादिष्ट होगा। दाल-पीठी मन्दी आँच पर थोड़ा-थोड़ा घी डाल कर देर तक भूनना चाहिए।

आइसक्रीम

आइसक्रीम कई प्रकार से बनायी जाती है। यहाँ तीन अच्छे फार्मूले दिये जा रहे हैं:

आइसक्रीम

सामग्री

½ लीटर दूध

कस्टर्ड पाउडर

½ किलो चीनी

2-3 अण्डे

100 ग्राम क्रीम

कॉफी/चॉकलेट पाउडर

चुटकी भर नमक

। चम्मच जिलेटिन

विधि

फार्मूला 1: आधा लीटर दूध में आधा पैकेट कस्टर्ड पाउडर से कस्टर्ड बनाइए। ठण्डा कीजिए। एक बड़े आम का गूदा मथकर या चार छोटे आमों का रस निकालकर मिलाइए। एक चम्मच जिलेटिन दो चम्मच गरम पानी में घोलकर उसे ठण्डा कीजिए व इस मिश्रण में मिला दीजिए। अन्दाज से चीनी मिलाकर फेंटिए और फ्रिज में जमने के लिए रख दीजिए। एक घण्टे बाद निकालिए। 100 ग्राम मलाई फेंटकर या क्रीम मिलाइए, पूरे मिश्रण को दोबारा फेंटिए व जमने के लिए फ्रिज में रख दीजिए।

फार्मूला 2: एक कप कॉफी बनाकर ठण्डी कीजिए या चॉकलेट पाउडर घोलकर ठण्डा कीजिए। एक कप मलाई पहले से तैयार रखिए। तीन अण्डे की जर्दी लेकर उन्हें हल्का फेंटिए। एक कप चीनी और चुटकीभर नमक मिलाकर इसमें आधा कप मलाई और कॉफी या चॉकलेट का घोल मिलाइए और फेंटिए। इस मिश्रण को भाप में पका लीजिए। ठण्डा करके शेष आधा कप मलाई मिलाइए व फिर फेंटिए। अब फ्रिज में जमने के लिए रख दीजिए।

फार्मूला 3: आधे लीटर दूध में दो अण्डों की जर्दी फेंटकर कस्टर्ड बनाइए। चीनी मिलाकर ठण्डा कीजिए। 100 ग्राम क्रीम फेंटकर मिलाइए। पूरे मिश्रण को फिर फेंटिए। एक चम्मच जिलेटिन को दो चम्मच गरम पानी में घोलकर ठण्डा कीजिए और मिश्रण में मिला दीजिए। फ्रिज में रखिए। एक घण्टे बाद तीन चौथाई जम जाने पर बाहर निकालिए। अण्डे की बची हुई सफेदी फेंटकर इसमें मिलाइए और आइसक्रीम को दोबारा फेंटिए। अब फिर जमने रख दीजिए। डेढ़-दो घण्टे बाद बढ़िया आइसक्रीम तैयार मिलेगी।

आइसक्रीम को कपों में डालकर 'क्रेप वैफर्स' के साथ सजाकर परोसिए।

कुछ टिप्स

ठण्डी आइसक्रीम पर चॉकलेट सिरप डाल
कर परोसें।

कुल्फी

गरमी के मौसम में ठण्डी कुल्फी खाने का मजा ही अलग होता है।

कुल्फी

सामग्री

1 लीटर दूध
½ कप चीनी
½ कप मेवे (कटे हुए)
1 चम्मच गुलाब जल
½ नींबू

विधि

एक लीटर दूध को औटाकर मन्दी आँच पर इतना गाढ़ा करें कि आधा रह जाये। या एक कप दूध और एक कप फेंटी हुई मलाई मिला लीजिए। इसमें आधा कप चीनी, कतरे मेवे, दो चम्मच गुलाब-जल या कुछ बून्द एसेंस मिलाइए। छोटा नींबू आधा या बड़ा एक चौथाई निचोड़कर मिलाइए फिर मिश्रण को साँचों में भरकर गुँथे आटे या मैदे से सील करके फ्रिज में रख दीजिए। (नींबू का रस मिलाने से 'क्रिस्टल्स' नहीं आयेंगे) कुछ समय बाद बढ़िया कुल्फी तैयार मिलेगी। फ्रिज न हो तो एक मटकी में बर्फ के टुकड़े भरकर नमक डाल दें व बर्फ के बीच कुल्फी के साँचे दबा दें। कुछ समय बाद मटकी को पकड़कर बार-बार हिलाइए। कुल्फी जम जायेगी।

कुछ टिप्स

कुल्फी बनाते समय कण्डेंस दूध डालने से कुल्फी गाढ़ी जमती है।

फ्रूट कस्टर्ड

भोजन के बाद देने के लिए यह एक लोकप्रिय 'स्वीट डिश' है।

सामग्री

- १ लीटर दूध
- १ कप कस्टर्ड पाउडर
- १ कप कटे हुए फल
- १ चम्मच गुलाब जल

फ्रूट कस्टर्ड

विधि

एक पैकेट कस्टर्ड पाउडर आधा कप पानी में घोलिए। आधा लीटर दूध उबालकर उसमें यह घोल छोड़कर चलाइए। गाढ़ा हो जाने पर चीनी मिलाकर उतार लीजिए। अंगूर के दाने और कटे हुए फल (सेब, नाशपाती, चीकू, केला, पपीता आदि) एक डोंगे में बिछाइए, उस पर कस्टर्ड की एक तह लगाइए। फिर फलों की इसी तरह तीन-चार तहें लगाकर डोंगा भरिए और उठाकर फ्रिज में रख दीजिए। थोड़ा गुलाबजल भी चाहें तो मिला सकती हैं। फ्रिज के बिना भी ठण्डी जगह रखकर कुछ समय बाद कस्टर्ड आपको जमा हुआ मिलेगा।

कुछ टिप्स

फ्रिज में रखने के बाद कई बार कस्टर्ड ज्यादा गाढ़ा हो जाता है। ऐसे में कस्टर्ड के अन्दर १-२ चम्मच ठण्डा दूध डालकर चम्मच से भली प्रकार मिला दें।

फ्रूट क्रीम

भोजन के बाद ठण्डी फ्रूट क्रीम खाने का मजा ही कुछ और होता है।

फ्रूट क्रीम

सामग्री

1 कप फेंटी हुई क्रीम

1 कप मिले-जुले फल (कटे हुए)

1 चम्मच गुलाबजल

1 चम्मच छिले हुए बादाम

5-6 चेरी

विधि

मौसम के अनुसार तथा आसानी से पाये जानेवाले फलो को चुनें जैसे कि पपीता, आम, लीची, अंगूर आदि। इन सभी फलों को धोकर बीजवाले फलों में से बीज निकालकर, उन्हें छोटे-छोटे टुकड़ों में काटें। फिर दूध से बना हुआ ताजा क्रीम या बाजार से क्रीम खरीदकर, उसे फलों के साथ मिलायें। कुछ देर फ्रीज़र में रखें। सजावट के लिए सलाद के ऊपर चेरी सा स्ट्रोबेरी लगायें और काँच के छोटे बर्तन में परोसें।

कुछ टिप्स

फ्रूट क्रीम को विशिष्ट काँच के कपों में ही परोसें।

पोटैटो चॉकलेट पुडिंग

आलू और चॉकलेट की यह पुडिंग अनोखी है।

पोटैटो चॉकलेट पुडिंग

सामग्री

125 ग्राम आलू

2 अण्डे

25 ग्राम कुकिंग चॉकलेट

60 ग्राम मक्खन

3 छोटे चम्मच कार्नफ्लोर

¼ छोटी चम्मच बेकिंग पाउडर

2 इलायची

कतरे हुए मेवे

चैरी (अन्दाज से)

विधि

आलू उबालकर छीलिए और मसल लीजिए। चॉकलेट और कार्नफ्लोर थोड़े पानी में फेंटकर दूध मिलाइए। अण्डों को फेंटकर थोड़ा-थोड़ा करके मिलाइए और फेंटती जाइए। चीनी मिला लीजिए। अब मक्खन और कुचले हुए आलू भी मिला लीजिए। कतरे मेवे, कुटी इलायची मिलाइए और यह मिश्रण एक बन्द डिब्बी में भरकर भाप में पकाइए। कुकर में दो कप पानी डालिए। ग्रिड (जाली) रखकर उस पर पुडिंग की डिब्बी रखिए। कुकर बन्द कर प्रेशर आने के बाद 20 मिनट तक पकाइए। ओवन में बेक भी कर सकती हैं। तैयार हो जाने पर निकालकर चैरी से सजाइए।

कुछ टिप्स

इस पुडिंग को ओवन में बेक भी कर सकते हैं।

In loving memory of my brother Nick, who journeyed the path with me in those early days and helped me remember the many experiences we shared during our childhood.

And in loving memory of the furry family members whose love and presence blessed my life in ways I could not have imagined—Sandy, Princess, and Jada—you are forever in my heart.

I would like to thank:

My wife Catherine, for all the countless hours of encouragement, resources, writing, and many years of real-life healing opportunities and experiences she gives me.

My daughter Zoe, for the many hours of reading, editing, and inspiration.

My daughter Ereca, for her insightful suggestions and encouragement to keep going.

My daughter Nicole, for her positive energy and willingness to reconnect.

My son Alexander, for taking the time out of his busy schedule to help me with reading, editing, and book cover input.

My son Mikey, for his positive thoughts and encouragement.

My siblings, without all the shared experiences, there would be no book. Some of you have been very supportive, I thank you!

My parents, for the gifts of music, languages, and life lessons.

Those relatives who played supportive roles in our lives, including our step-father.

Those family and friends from my past who taught me valuable lessons about love and forgiveness; especially Joe & Lorraine, Jay & Edie, Dale & Ellen, Marvin & Joanie and Dr. John.

The Grandparents, who continuously show their love and support to our family. Andi & Marvin, Jenny & Larry.

Brian B., for his insights about book titles and the writing process.

Cameron, for always being positive about the book's possibilities.

A special thanks to my good friend and accountability partner, Annie, for her encouragement and insights throughout the years.

A special thanks to Benecia Ponder, my primary editor; this book wouldn't have been possible without her patience, understanding, and talent for taking my story and creating a book that would be easy to read and understand. I was divinely guided to work with her and the experience has been awesome. I look forward to working with her again in the future.

The Illumination Press team, for all their hard work to help make this book a success.

My Divine Creator, for the guidance I received while writing. There were many times that I felt like giving up, but I was encouraged by a greater power of love that kept me going. I am forever grateful.

Myself, for not giving up amidst the self-doubt, insecurities, and fears about writing this book. I am grateful for the lessons and healing I gained along the way.

I believe everyone has a story to tell. I encourage anyone who wants to write a book to show up and let the process unfold.

Good Luck & God Bless!

Foreword

The Healing Space is brilliantly written as a guide to bring the reader through a series of exercises and guided moments of meditation to find that special place—the Healing Space—where the wounded Inner-Child meets the Higher-Self. That special place where healing begins and continues. That special place where you realize that love and forgiveness is not necessarily how to love and forgive another person, but how to love and forgive yourself, to uplift that wounded self into loving oneself, and forgiving one's self.

Dr. Ergas's book helps you to realize that there is a place that exists where healing occurs, and it all happens within yourself. He guides the reader to realize that you, the reader, are the actual healer, and that love, for one's self, is the power to heal past traumas and current unconscious patterns.

It is the ability to truly love one's self that finally allows us to love others.

It is through the power of this self love that allows us to heal ourselves and others, even allowing us to create space for healing in our family relationships, past and present, and creating a current family of love.

I have known Dr. Ergas for many years, not just as a colleague, but as a healer, a teacher, a walking encyclopedia of knowledge that could have any search engine respond with more questions than answers. His knowledge, plus experience, brings about a wisdom that rarely has a parallel to compare to him. His compassion and love for people is beyond exceptional in comparison to other doctors and healers. I see it every week on the faces of people he has worked with in healing sessions. His energy is tranquil, supportive, loving and safe. Not to mention, his ability to nurture the plants in our office back to health is outstanding.

Should you find yourself ready to start this healing journey, ready to heal yourself and others, I strongly recommend The Healing Space as your source for guidance. His journey of exploration is timeless. His personal stories have a tendency to mirror so many others' stories of overcoming childhood traumas, adult traumas, or any traumatic experiences, as if you were reading about yourself. He shares the necessary tools required to acknowledge, heal and create new experiences.

Take your time working through each chapter. Don't try to use the work all in one day or one weekend. Give yourself the love and the space to work through each chapter individually. Allow yourself to integrate these new experiences. Then you will find how each step blends itself into a unique healing journey, all together.

Abundant Blessings Always & All Ways,
Dr. Cynthia Seebacher, D.C., LMT, BS Ed

Table of Contents

Acknowledgments i

Foreward v

Introduction
The Day My Inner Child Met My Higher Self 01

Chapter One:
Love, The Greatest Healer of All................................ 11

Chapter Two:
Love Is a Memory that Time Cannot Change.......................... 19

Chapter Three:
Divine Love 27

Chapter Four:
Loving Your Uniqueness................................... 35

Chapter Five:
A Love Story................................... 43

Chapter Six:
Roadblocks to Love 51

Chapter Seven:
The Power of Forgiveness................................... 65

Chapter Eight:
Family, Creating Love's Blueprint (For Better or Worse).......... 73

Chapter Nine:
Nourishing Your Soul 83

ChapterTen:
What's Love Got to Do with It? (Everything).......................... 91

Final Words of Encouragement 109

Meet the Author 115

The Day My Inner Child Met My Higher Self

This part of my journey begins on a sunny summer afternoon, deep in a heartfelt conversation with a new referral. As usual, I introduced our session by painting a picture of the transformative journey we were about to embark on.

I explained to her that an energy session is like a soothing symphony, where your body and spirit are the instruments. It's a time for surrendering yourself to a state of complete relaxation, finding safety and serenity in a sacred space. The purpose of this ritual is to bridge the gap between the Inner Child and the Higher Self - two parts of our soul that often become estranged from the many challenges found in life.

The Inner Child, who has been bruised and silenced by past trauma, is given a chance to connect with the Higher Self - a beacon of wisdom and enlightenment. This union illuminates the dark corners of the heart, enabling the healing process to begin.

The journey begins with a countdown from ten to zero, called grounding. This allows you to anchor yourself firmly in the present moment while mindful breathing guides you into a deep state of tranquility. Your attention gently guides you to scan your body while quiet affirmations echo in your ears. The mantras vibrate through your being while harmonious sounds of water and nature wrap you in a calming lullaby. The flickering candles and the comfortable warmth of the room further add to the ambiance and experience.

This hallowed atmosphere where the Inner Child and Higher Self meet is the Healing Space-the crucible where all energetic healing occurs. Here, the Higher Self brings clarity to the Inner Child, guiding them through the emotional process of releasing the shackles that have kept the child anchored in past traumas. It is also here that the Inner Child learns to embrace Love and Trust, stepping bravely into the next chapter of their existence. This space hums with Divine energy, offering a sanctuary of peace and spiritual bliss where true healing unfolds.

Having walked her through this sacred process, she was eager to begin our energetic session toward healing. As she found her grounding, I invited her to envision a mesmerizing landscape adorned with vibrant flowers and lush trees; this was a safe haven where the sun's gentle rays filtered through the leafy canopy above, and cast a warm, comforting glow. The whispers of a gentle breeze carried secrets from a nearby pond, its surface shimmering like a mirror under the sun's caress. We experienced sweet melodies of nature - the birds' symphonies, the rustling of the leaves - all wrapped in the intoxicating scent of gardenias and honeysuckles. This serene scene offered a profound sense of safety and tranquility, paving the way toward self-discovery and healing.

As we dove into the visualization of her wounded Inner Child, she began to paint a vivid picture of her past. Her words flowed like a river, revealing painful memories of abuse from her father and betrayal by her mother. As she wept, reliving these agonizing moments, I called upon her Higher Self and Spirit Guides to assist us in this healing journey.

But then, something unexpected happened. I found myself instantly in two places-between guiding her and traveling on my own path. My consciousness wandered back to my Inner Child at the tender age of 9 or 10. I observed him standing there, tears streaming down his face, a portrait of sorrow and loneliness. His words echoed through my mind, revealing a deeply rooted belief that he was unloved and that despite his best efforts, he could never please his parents.

At that moment-my Higher Self stepped forward, meeting my Inner Child's gaze with a gentle yet firm resolve. With a voice full of compassion and wisdom, my Higher Self reassured the young boy, "You are not alone. You are cherished by the many who journey with us on our path. I want you to understand that those traumas and hardships you faced back then were not your fault. You are a remarkable, loving soul, respected and loved by all who know you. The scars of your past no longer hold you captive. I, your Higher Self, have risen above many of the trials of abuse, neglect, and abandonment and have come to reconnect with you so you, too, can be freed from the bonds of our past."

After this shared experience of revisiting, accepting, and letting go of some of our sorrowful past, a sense of relief washed over us with a calm assurance that we had released some of the chains of our past. With a heartfelt smile, my Higher Self reached out to my Inner Child, took him by the hand, and whispered, "It's safe to grow up now. You are safe with me. I love you. Let's continue moving through life together." Their smiles mirrored each other as they embarked on a shared path towards healing, with a new found passion for becoming the best version of themselves.

Returning to the present moment, I was surprised and thankful for what came next. As I concluded the session with my client, she said. "That was one of the best sessions I've ever experienced." With a wide-eyed grin, I replied, "I couldn't agree more."

In the quiet stillness that followed that profound session, I retreated into a cocoon of introspection. It was a moment of revelation when I discovered that my Inner Child had been frozen in time at the tender age of nine. While delving into those memories, the reason why became clear to me.

Memories of tip-toeing on eggshells and living in constant fear of triggering an eruption of anger surfaced like shadows from the past. I remembered the delicate dance of caution we performed while anticipating the sting of both emotional and physical punishment. The dread that brewed with something as trivial as accidentally spilling mommy's coffee was palpable. The ritual of selecting the proper switch from the cherry bush was an exercise in cruelty. The horror of watching her strip the leaves off, making sure it wasn't brittle or prone to snapping.

It needed to bend and swish while cutting through the air, enough to leave behind painful welts and sometimes draw blood. The truth is, the sound alone triggered the intense fear of dread and pain. If the chosen switch didn't meet these harsh criteria, or you tried to avoid getting hit, or cried, the punishment would escalate. One of Mommy's famous sayings: "If you cry, I'll give you something to cry for."

The echoes of ceaseless arguments filled with threats of abandonment and talks of divorce reverberated in my mind. The hollow feeling of being unloved, unwanted, and viewed as nothing more than a burden on my parents' lives was a constant companion during those years. Daily existence was fraught with the threat of being cast aside, left to fend for myself in a world that seemed so vast and unforgiving.

Memories of hunger gnawed at me. Recollections of wearing hand-me-down, worn-out clothes and shoes with holes in them were poignant reminders of our humble existence. The sadness and fear I experienced were often more for my siblings than for me, as some of them got into more trouble than I did. For example, I never got back-fisted in the face like some of my brothers did.

Our stepfather's entry into our lives intensified this dysfunctional home life; his physical abuse towards our mother and us added another layer of torment. Our challenge was not just to survive but to endure the mental, physical, emotional, and for some, sexual abuse. Amidst this turmoil, we lost our grandmother, who was the one ray of sunshine in our otherwise cloudy existence. It was a devastating blow to us all, as we no longer had her support or protection.

As the veil of introspection lifted, I gently returned to the present, cradling a profound sense of tranquility. Yet, nestled within that calm was a burgeoning sense of responsibility and determination - an earnest desire to guide others toward healing from the wounds that mirrored my own childhood traumas. Questions about my healing journey began to dance on the edges of my consciousness, probing whether I had ventured far enough along this path or if there was still more work to do. I wanted to commune with my inner child again to ensure that we were in harmony as we moved toward our shared destination. Despite the solitude that enveloped me, I longed for this support with my entire being.

Since that transformative moment, as I have grown toward understanding and healing my own Inner Child, I find myself better equipped to guide others along their path. My newly found mission was (and still is)-to help others discover their Healing Space, find answers to some of their life's questions, and guide them toward a clearer vision of their chosen path. This meditative process requires having the right mindset, guided breathing, focused attention, body scanning, mantra repetition, reflection, and an attitude of gratitude. It's about living in love and trust and letting go of fear and doubt. Without having the right mindset, it's very challenging to overcome trauma. I recommend working with highly trained professionals like Psychotherapists, Counselors, and Energy Healers who can meet you where you are and guide you where you want to go.

We all, at some point in our lives, encounter some form of trauma. As children, we wrestle with understanding why misfortune befalls even the most virtuous among us. We struggle to comprehend how those entrusted with our care can sometimes be agents of abuse, neglect, and abandonment. I have learned that these traumatic experiences can anchor us to our past, and prevent us from fully embracing life until we confront and resolve them.

When the Inner Child and the Higher Self unite, the Inner Child is enlightened with a deep comprehension of past traumas. The Higher Self reveals how these experiences disempowered the Inner Child and conveys the knowledge needed to move forward. This union marks a pivotal step in the healing process; it allows them to merge into a singular, empowered entity and initiates a powerful cycle of healing and progression as they march steadfastly towards becoming their best self.

When assisted by your Higher Self and Higher Power, you have the Spiritual guidance necessary to succeed.

"Go often to your Healing Space, which lies deep within your heart; for there you will find no questions, only answers." Dr. Mitch Ergas

As you delve into this book, I want you to know that you are not alone. We all wrestle with life's challenges, occasionally finding ourselves in dark corners and grappling with feelings of despair. But remember, there is always hope. Just as I managed to rise above my circumstances and move forward, so can you. I share my story as a beacon of hope to inspire resilience and the courage to stand up again, release the past, and keep moving forward. I hope by reading this book, you will find the inspiration–to give life and love another chance, to discover or rediscover this healing power. Please remember that your past doesn't define you, It merely serves as a stepping stone to who you can become.

The Self-Help tools, techniques, steps, and stories in this book can help to inspire and motivate you to take the necessary action steps for healing and forward movement on your road to Self-Mastery.

What you can learn as you journey through this Book:

> **Chapter 1—THE GREATEST HEALER OF ALL**—Guides you through a six-question and answer process of self-reflection about the healing power of love and its role in your life. Your answers can bring clarity and inspire you to take action.

> **Chapter 2—LOVE IS A MEMORY THAT TIME CANNOT CHANGE**—You will learn 5 powerful steps to help you experience the joy of giving and receiving love. You will also receive examples of some of the many Negative Repetitive Patterns that keep you

stuck and some solutions for correcting them. This chapter also provides some question-and-answer insight you will discover during the process.

Chapter 3—DIVINE LOVE—One of my favorite ways to learn comes through personal stories. This chapter is just that. Enjoy it and find the parts that resonate with you, then apply the lessons to your own life.

Chapter 4—LOVING YOUR UNIQUENESS—I share my Roadmap, an 8-step guide that will illuminate your path toward self-transformation and healing.

Chapter 5—A LOVE STORY— Shares a powerful personal story about the loss of love and the healing power of closure. It also contains some excellent quotations about love that have been an inspiration to me. Quotations can be powerful thought stimulators that can motivate and inspire others.

Chapter 6—ROADBLOCKS TO LOVE—You will learn 5 specific roadblocks, how they hold you back, and what you need to overcome them, along with six questions that will help you to recognize when you need to take action. The P.O.E Technique is included at the end of this chapter as a Bonus gift from above during one of the darkest periods of my life. You will learn the technique and how to use it. It is for those stressful periods in your life when you have to function quickly!

Chapter 7—THE POWER OF FORGIVENESS.—Includes a 7-question/ answer session about the healing power of forgiveness and how it opens valuable doors necessary for personal growth and development. This process ties into other chapters and helps you to utilize the power of forgiveness for yourself and others.

Chapter 8—FAMILY, CREATING LOVE'S BLUEPRINT (FOR BETTER OR WORSE)—Helps you to identify early blueprint traits, how they affect you, and possible solutions for creating healthier ones. Doing the work necessary to change these traits, can bring greater happiness. Resource information, including a link for this material, is provided. A few of my favorite quotes about the importance of family are shared. I hope that these thoughts will resonate with and inspire you.

Chapter 9—NOURISHING YOUR SOUL—In this chapter, you will learn 8-ways to nourish your soul. These are the tools that I use and have shared with family and friends with great success. I am confident that if you implement them into your life, you will find them to be just as powerful for you.

Chapter 10—WHAT'S LOVE GOT TO DO WITH IT? In the final chapter of this book, you are given 6 Transformation Challenges and some of their possible solutions to work with. Some of my favorite resources listed there as well.

Please remember: when someone asks you, "What's love got to do with it", be sure to respond "Everything!"

Chapter One

Love,
The Greatest
Healer of All

From the tender years of my early childhood, I was shaped by a powerful contrast of influences - those that fostered images of positivity and others that bred little besides negativity. It was this dichotomy, this interplay of light and shadow, that crafted the core beliefs that would guide me through life's labyrinth of challenges and opportunities.

When I delve into the realms of love, my grandmother's voice echoes in my heart. My memories are of her speaking of a profound love for Jesus. She illuminated the depth of a love so vast that He willingly sacrificed His life for all humanity. To comprehend such an act of crucifixion and suffering He endured was to grapple with a love beyond human understanding.

"Why?" I would question her. "Why would anyone choose this path?"

Her answer was simple yet profound. "Because He loves us, and wants to offer us redemption from our sins." she said.

As a child, I also questioned what sins I needed forgiveness for. I was raised under the strict and persuasive guidance of my mother and grandmother. They instilled in us the understanding that we all make mistakes, and it's through repentance that we can rectify them. Having faith that I was divinely connected to a Higher Power, made me want to become the best version of myself. Yet, like most people, I had years of uncertainty and missteps.

For a few years, my family attended weekly meetings. Later, I continued this tradition alone, finding solace and connection within the spiritual community. During my high school years, I veered off the well-trodden path, stepping into a season of exploration and experimentation. My circle of friends ranged from those who were pillars of positive influence to those who journeyed alongside me on this path of self-discovery.

These formative years took place in the United States during the sixties and seventies, marked by the Vietnam War, peace protests, and cultural shifts. The anthem of our generation was one of anti-war sentiment, a call for freedom, and a melody carried forward by the iconic musicians and philosophers of the time.

This era was also marked by a wave of Flower Power and peace-loving hippies, a radical exploration of individual freedoms. Amidst all this, a desire emerged to discern the authentic from the superficial, a collective awakening towards self-realization.

We stood firm in our beliefs, influenced heavily by the Beatles, Dylan, Crosby, Stills, Nash, and Young, and other iconic bands of the day. Interestingly, even amidst our exploratory phase, we found ourselves deeply connected to our Divinity. This connection has guided many of us full circle. I am eternally grateful for those family members and friends who have positively influenced my life. Some of my most cherished memories are those shared with friends and loved ones-moments filled with laughter, song, and profound conversations about the purpose of life.

Many parents at the time were fraught with worry about their children being drafted into the war, while others planned for college or work after graduation. Our family lived in constant concern for my older brother Nick, who was serving in Vietnam. We prayed daily for his safety, a prayer that was thankfully answered. Our mother was deeply affected by the stress of his deployment, a burden she carried even after his safe return. Like all soldiers, Nicky paid a heavy price for his service, but he always felt protected by a Higher Power during his time there. While lying on his deathbed, he said he called upon God, promising to lead a life of kindness and service if he survived. His prayers were answered, and he returned home to embark on the next chapter of his life. We were immensely grateful that he made it back alive.

As I consider the totality of my life experiences, I can see the beauty in each one. Each stumble and triumph etched a blueprint in my mind and heart-one of faith in a force beyond my comprehension, a force greater than myself. This faith became my beacon of courage and a wellspring of hope. It whispered to me that no matter how treacherous the journey, no matter how steep the mountains or how deep the valleys, there was always a glimmer of hope at the end of the tunnel.

One principle that has been a guiding star for me is the Golden Rule: "Do unto others as you would have them do unto you."

This simple yet profound belief has taught me that love and acceptance are not just virtues but necessities. By embracing this rule, I've learned that showing love to others is not just an act of kindness but also a way to heal ourselves. It offers us the opportunity to help others navigate their own healing process from the traumas and emotional wounds life invariably inflicts upon us all. One of my favorite stories about love and forgiveness is found in the Bible. A man's youngest son asks for his inheritance and runs off to spend it frivolously. By the time he has nothing left and nowhere to go, he returns home to an older brother, angry with him for selfishness. His father, however, sees his regret and welcomes him home with open arms and forgiveness. The story of the Prodigal Son, helps me to realize that we all have free agency to choose our own paths and that sometimes the choices we make have detrimental consequences. It also teaches the importance of not judging others when they make poor choices that hurt themselves. We can also learn the importance of forgiveness and unconditional love from this story. I know that many of us have been in this situation at some point in our lives. This story gives powerful insight into handling similar situations, whether it's with family or close friends.

The lessons from this story have deeply ingrained in me the understanding that **"Love is the greatest healer of all."**

And with that, I invite you to ponder, reflect, and answer these questions. There is no right or wrong answer, just a simple exercise to get you thinking about the healing power of love.

- How has love healed you?

- When have you witnessed the healing power of love in someone else?

- How can you harness the power of love to heal yourself and assist others with their healing process?

- How were you able to love yourself during the times you were down on yourself?

- Do you connect to a Higher Power, Universe, best friend, or family member when you need to feel loved?

- What are your core beliefs around loving others and being loved?

As you continue your journey of healing and growth, read and reread your answers to the above questions for guidance. In them, you can find some solutions. You will find more tools and techniques as you continue your journey through the book.

Remember that Love is the Greatest Healer of all, and in the words of Sri Sri Ravi Shankar, "Find the love you seek, by first finding the love within yourself. Learn to rest in that place within you that is your true home."

Once you can do this, you can then share your love with others. I often read quotations as they inspire me to keep moving forward. Here are a few of my favorite quotes about love. Hopefully, they will inspire you as well.

♥

"I love you not because of who you are but
because of who I am when I'm with you."
Roy Croft

♥

"You are my sun, my moon, and all my stars."
e.e. Cummings

♥

"I knew I loved you before I met you."
Savage Garden

♥

"Love is patient, love is kind. It does not boast.
It is not proud."
The Bible

♥

"All you need is Love."
The Beatles

♥

♥

"Greater love hath no man than this, that a man lay down his life for his friends."
Jesus

♥

"When you love yourself, and love others as much as you love yourself; it opens the door for others to love you. Love resonates with Love!"
Dr. Mitch Ergas

♥

Chapter Two

Love Is a Memory that Time Cannot Change

In the darkest times, when hope seems like a distant memory, remember this: Love and Trust are potent forces that can bring about unimaginable transformations, even miracles. I've lived through such moments, when the light at the end of the tunnel was barely visible, yet still there. These experiences often revolved around painful separations from loved ones I held dear. Yet, in those trying times, I discovered the power of Faith and Hope and the magic they can weave when coupled with earnest prayer.

There were instances when the people I yearned for were no longer in my life. We were separated by the harsh realities of divorce, abandonment, and adoption. Despite these challenging circumstances, astonishing outcomes unfolded as if a divine intervention was at play. It felt like my guardian angels and spirit guides were listening to my heart's pleas, extending their celestial assistance to comfort and guide me.

One such profound experience involved my eldest daughter, Nicole.

After high school graduation, I felt life calling me towards the West Coast. My brother John, my friend Jimmy and I set off for our new adventure. We left Florida and went to Georgia on our way Westward. We decided to earn money for the trip by working at a family restaurant. We had a lot of fun immersing ourselves in the rich culture of this Greek restaurant-The Golden Dolphin, where my Aunt Mary and Uncle George were the proud owners. The food was divine and the music soulful, especially when my friend George Soffos, a Bouzouki player of unmatched talent, took the stage. He was the Eric Clapton of his instrument. Those were joyous times as we saved our earnings for our dream journey, all while basking in the beauty of the Middle Eastern languages and my Greek Heritage.

The West Coast greeted us with its charm, and after juggling various jobs, I found a purpose that resonated with me - becoming a hairdresser and make-up artist. This journey took me to beauty school, and around this time, I crossed paths with a beautiful young woman. She had a heart of gold and worked at a grocery store nearby. Her conservative and religious upbringing didn't deter our connection, and we decided to tie the knot to continue our relationship. However, our union was short-lived. I was not ready to settle down, and my lack of emotional maturity led to our separation.

Our brief union blessed us with a beautiful daughter, Nicole, a name we both loved. Unfortunately, life had different plans, and I lost touch with Nicole. I was young and naïve, and under the guidance of someone I trusted, was encouraged to give up my parental rights because of their religious beliefs. Being young, not fully understanding their process, and not wanting to create problems; I walked away. This decision, a regrettable mistake of my youth, caused me immense emotional pain. I longed for a connection with Nicole and prayed for her daily well-being.

After losing touch with Nicole when she was merely an infant, I never stopped wanting to connect with her. Her memory remained etched in my soul, a constant reminder of the love that never faded. Day after day, night after night, my thoughts would drift to her, and my prayers would ascend, filled with hopes of reconnection. The guilt, shame, and fear of rejection I felt was so overwhelming that it kept me from reaching out.

My dear mother, in her wisdom and love, made me promise something before she departed from this world. She asked me to never give up on Nicole, to keep the flame of hope alive. She also urged me to maintain close ties with my siblings. It was a promise I easily gave, for it resonated deeply within me, echoing my own long-held desires.

So, even when time stretches out, creating vast chasms between our present and our past, the memories of love remain undiminished. Time may alter many things, but the love we hold in our hearts is impervious to its passage.

The guilt of abandoning Nicole haunted me, reminding me of my father who had abandoned me. It was a painful void that nothing could fill, especially during special milestones and holidays that I knew I was missing with her. Despite my love for her, I had failed to express it and still feel guilty about it.

In search of healing and love, I turned to spirituality. I immersed myself in religious, philosophical, and self-help books. My spiritual journey led me into various relationships and eventually to my current partner, who helped me to understand the challenges of both giving and receiving love. I have learned valuable lessons from each relationship that I have been in, and I am grateful for them all.

Here are five things that have helped me experience the joy of giving and receiving love. I believe they will help you with your healing process as well. Think about the questions listed below, answer them, and then apply what you learn to the appropriate areas of your life.

1. **Be open.** To give or receive something you must first open your hand. Notice if there is a part of you trying to protect yourself from getting hurt by not opening up. Once you have been hurt, it is harder to open up the second time-but important to do so. You cannot move forward when your heart is closed off.

2. **Love is a verb.** Once you are open to the process, be willing to express love. Practice this with your family, friends, and anyone that you feel is in need. Be sure to include yourself, as you could be the one lacking the love you need. Start by doing something special for yourself, treat yourself to a nice dinner, or check something off of your bucket list. Positive self-talk is a good start.

3. **Forgiveness is crucial.** Be sure to give and receive forgiveness with real intent. This process is needed to let go of stored, negative energy. Only by forgiving and being forgiven can the

door to healing open. Be positive, humble, and sincere in your approach. Most of all, remember to forgive yourself, which can be the most challenging and rewarding part.

4. **Letting Go of Fear and Doubt.** Sometimes, letting go of Fear and Doubt requires deep work, especially where there has been trauma. Replacing Fear and Doubt with Love and Trust is essential to begin the healing cycle. I often work with clients who need healing on deeper levels. This process of energy work is called Energetic Therapeutics. For temporary help in letting go quickly, use The P.O.E. Technique found at the end of Chapter Six listed as a Bonus.

5. **Gratitude is essential.** Be thankful for being able to give to others and grateful when others give to you. Notice the joy of giving and receiving and how it blesses everyone involved. Be thankful for everything, everyone, and for all the gifts, talents, and abilities you have. You can demonstrate this by thinking of others and through simple acts of kindness. Sharing an honest "thank you" holds more value than you could imagine. An attitude of gratitude can open many doors and windows of opportunities for you.

Life is indeed a journey, and mine has been a roller coaster of emotions and experiences. But as I have discovered - Love is a memory that time cannot change, and in my case, absence did make the heart grow fonder.

As you continue your journey, reflect on these questions and your answers while considering what we discussed above.

There are no right or wrong answers. By doing so, you will gain a deeper understanding of the process of giving and receiving love.

1. Have you ever experienced a time when Love and Trust transformed a seemingly hopeless situation?

2. Can you recall those moments when Faith and Hope guided you through a challenging time?

3. How have the memories of love helped you navigate through life's trials?

4. What promises have you made that resonate deeply with your own desires?

5. How has the enduring nature of love inspired or guided you on your journey?

6. In the past, what challenges have you faced with the love process?

As you embrace the changes needed to give and receive love openly, experiment with the ways that come naturally to you; do not try to force the issue, as this creates Fear and Doubt. Try using an approach that incorporates Love and Trust. Can you remember a moment in time where you felt emotionally connected to giving or receiving love? By focusing on the energy of your feelings, you can reignite your passion and open your mind and heart to new ones. When this happens, you quickly realize that **Love Is a Memory that Time Cannot Change.**

Chapter Three

Divine Love

In the grand, intricate tapestry of life, we each occupy a unique space. Our backgrounds are as varied as the threads that weave this complex pattern. Some of us hail from humble beginnings, others from more affluent circumstances. Despite these differences- there is a universal truth that binds us all: we are not alone in our journey.

Many of us, in our own way, are deeply connected to an ever-present Higher Power, a force that transcends our human understanding.

As an individual, I am a fervent believer in a Higher Power. It is a conviction that has grown stronger in me with each passing year. It is rooted in personal experiences, introspection, and countless conversations with loved ones. To me, it is an embodiment of pure love. It knows us intimately - every thought, every desire, every fear - and walks with us through the various seasons of our lives. It celebrates our triumphs, comforts us in our sorrows, and guides us when we feel lost.

This Higher Power goes by many names across different cultures and religions - God, the Universe, Allah, Jesus, Buddha, Krishna, Abraham, Divine Creator, etc. I believe what truly matters is belief, the faith that there is a power greater than ourselves; a Divine Being that loves us unconditionally and guides us on our path. The name is not as important as faith itself. To me, faith is a beacon of hope and strength during times of adversity. Life is a symphony of experiences; a harmonious blend of laughter, tears, triumphs, and trials. Through the countless conversations I've shared with friends and family and the moments of joy and sorrow I've experienced with them over the years, I have come to understand an important truth: it is during our darkest hours, when despair casts a long shadow over our hearts, that a Higher Power offers us solace and strength.

This Higher Power of Divine Love, is an unseen force, as mysterious as it is comforting. It's like an invisible hand that gently guides us through the storms of life, an ever-present companion that whispers words of encouragement when we feel lost. This profound sentiment is beautifully expressed in the poem "Footprints in the Sand" by Margaret F. Powers. Inspired by a Biblical verse, the poem serves as a poignant reminder of the enduring love and compassion that our Higher Power bestows upon us.

A person is walking along the beach one night when scenes of their life begin flashing through their mind. During the vision two sets of footprints are seen in the sand. In the darkest moments of this person's life there was only one set of footprints in the sand. "Lord, why was there only one set of footprints in the sand." He replied that "those were the times that I carried you." It is comforting for me to think that we are not alone!

Now, let me share a pearl of wisdom from a woman who is an inspiration to many, including myself: Oprah Winfrey. She once said, "The whole point of being alive is to evolve into the person you were meant to be."

How true these words ring out to me!

We are all works in progress, constantly evolving and growing. I firmly believe that Divine Love is an expression of our Higher Power that fuels this transformative journey.

In the grand scheme of life, love is the most potent force; the most precious gift. To love and be loved unconditionally. Isn't that the essence of our existence? Divine Love is the key that connects us to our Higher Power, and guides us toward becoming the best versions of ourselves.

As I journey through the vast landscape of life, guided by this compass. I utilize this sacred mantra. It's more than just a string of words; it's a philosophy, a way of life that echoes the principles of Divine Love.

It states,

"The love that unfolds in front of you daily is perfect. Embrace it, honor it, give thanks for it, and most of all; share it because, out of our everyday random acts of kindness and love, a greater love for everyone and everything around us is born."
(Dr. Mitch Ergas)

Each day, life presents us with countless opportunities to experience love: In the rising sun that bathes the world in its warm glow, in the gentle rustling of the leaves, in the whispering secrets of the wind, with the birth of a newborn, the laughter of children, the playfulness of our favorite pet, and in the comforting silence shared with a loved one. This love, unfolding in a myriad of forms, is flawless in its existence. It is a gift from the Divine; a blessing to be cherished.

Embracing this love means opening our hearts fully and allowing love to seep into every cell of our being. It means acknowledging love in all its forms, even when it arrives in unexpected packages. To honor love is to respect its power; its capacity to heal and transform. It's about recognizing love as the ultimate truth; the core essence of our existence.

One of my favorite quotes about love was by Mahatma Gandhi: "The day the power of love overrules the love of power, the world will know peace."

Yet, look at what is happening all over the world right now, wars and rumors of wars, with innocent men, women, and children being the unfortunate casualties. To get to peace, we must not just want peace and love, we must have a sincere desire for them, and live our lives as examples of it. We must express gratitude for it. Gratitude amplifies the power of love, creating a positive feedback loop of joy and contentment. When we are thankful for peace and love, we attract more of it into our lives. We have no power over other people and their greed for power and money; but we can pray for peace and be loving when and wherever possible. We live in challenging times, with stress all around us, but we need not focus on the negative stuff. Instead, focus on the things that bring you peace and love. As a wise man once said; "One of the greatest tragedies in life is worrying about things you have no control over." Patanjali.

Most importantly, do not bury your love. Each act of kindness, each word of compassion, and each gesture of love has the potential to ignite a spark of love in others. It is through these seemingly insignificant acts that a greater love is born. This is a love that envelopes everyone and everything around us.

This way of thinking serves as a gentle reminder to live each day in alignment with love. It encourages us to be conduits; to let love flow through us, touching the lives of those around us. Because, at the end of the day, we are all interconnected threads in the grand tapestry of life, woven together by the threads of this Divine Love.

Yet, sometimes we find ourselves struggling to access this. Often, as mentioned before, the key lies in the act of forgiveness-even when there has been wrongdoing by one or both parties. I know that this is no easy task! But it can pave the way for Divine Love to flow freely.

In such situations, I find it helpful to reverse roles - by putting myself in the shoes of the one who has wronged me. This perspective shift often grants me a deeper understanding and gives me the strength necessary to forgive. Holding onto grudges only breeds negativity, which can grow and manifest into physical and emotional ailments. On the other hand, letting go of them helps to heal and liberate everyone involved.

Sometimes, however, we might not receive forgiveness. In such instances, remember that the act of asking for forgiveness is, in itself, a step towards healing. If they choose not to forgive, the burden lies with them; as you have done all you can. In the intricate dance of life, two elements - love and forgiveness - are so deeply intertwined that their existence is mutually dependent. Forgiving someone, is not merely releasing resentment or bitterness; it's an act steeped in love. It's a testament to your heart's resilience and capacity to rise above pain and hurt.

I extend an invitation to you today: pause and reflect upon someone with whom you can exercise this noble art of forgiveness. Feel the burden of your past pain gradually lifting, replaced by a liberating lightness that fills your heart. This is the transformative power of letting go.

Blessings, like the rain, shower upon us from the heavens. Some fall freely, while others, require us to step out and open our hearts and hands to receive them. This delicate equilibrium represents Divine love: a system designed to stimulate growth and learning through our choices.

Free will is not a constraint, but an empowerment. It's a gift that lets you navigate life's labyrinth. We can learn lessons from our missteps and can grow from our experiences. Every decision we make, every path we tread, and every lesson we learn, are stepping stones towards becoming the best version of ourselves.

Eden Ahbez, a wise soul whose words have touched many hearts, once said, "The greatest thing you'll ever learn is just to love and be loved in return." These simple words, brimming with profound wisdom, remind us that love, in its purest form, is the essence of our existence. In my experience, this has been one of my life's greatest lessons.

As you journey through life, strive to be loving, forgiving and grateful. These three practices can help you to tap into the magic and beauty of living. There are many personal lessons you can learn as well as those of others. As you read through these chapters, you will discover additional tips and strategies to assist you along your healing path.

Chapter Four

Loving Your Uniqueness

In the innocence of my youth, I was often struck by how broad the scope of human existence was. The diverse accents, names, physical appearances, professions, and the glaring disparities in living conditions often sparked endless question and answer sessions between my family and friends. Why were some people clothed in rags, living in dilapidated homes with no sign of luxury, while others seemingly had everything - opulent homes, shiny toys, fashionable clothes, and an abundance of food and money?

Before I could fully comprehend the answers, I sought wisdom from my parents and grandparents. Among my earliest memories are the bitter lessons of our family's poverty. The constant reminder that my parents struggled to provide for us rang sharply in my ears. There was a perpetual shortage of food, money, and clothes. This narrative sowed seeds of inadequacy, guilt, and shame within me, fostering feelings of being unloved, unwanted, and less than.

As I wrestled with these feelings of inferiority, I clung to one of my father's cherished sayings: "From good people come good things." Over time, this mantra would help guide me through what seemed to be a never-ending struggle of self-doubt. It was at this time I began to focus on becoming the best version of myself.

Each of us must remember that we are unique, but this does not detract from our worth. Bullies often target those they perceive to be different or strange, and attempt to belittle them because they don't fit into societal norms. Childhood memories of being ridiculed for being different or poor, remain fresh in my mind. In response to bullying, my siblings and I built fantasy worlds where we could be anyone we dreamed of.

Our differences, whether socio-economic, ethnic, or stemming from our dysfunctional home life, often manifested as insecurity. Yet, these feelings did not define me. Instead, I learned to focus on the gifts, talents, and abilities bestowed upon me by my Divine Creator. I learned to appreciate my uniqueness, despite the world's insistence on conformity.

I firmly believe that the world would be a better place if people focused far less on our differences and much more on our shared humanity. You may not be able to change others, but you can change your own life, guiding yourself toward understanding and compassion. I remember the words of one of my greatest life teachers, Grandmaster Yin, whose philosophy was: "To improve the world around you, you must first improve yourself." This became the motto of a martial arts class I taught for years.

Despite our early adversities, my siblings and I found success in our chosen professions, a testament to our resilience and determination.

Regardless of your origins or differences, your Divine Creator has blessed each of you with unique talents and abilities. We all experience moments of self-doubt and self-confidence. Grandmaster Yin also said: "Kung-fu is knowing what to do in any given situation in life because you have developed your skills, talents, and abilities over a period of time." In challenging times, when feelings of insignificance creep in, it's helpful to remember your inherent worth by focusing on these things. Also, by seeking solace in a higher power through prayer and meditation, you can find peace and guidance on how to best utilize your uniqueness.

Just as we wish to alleviate the suffering of others, we must remember that we are divine beings capable of overcoming adversity. I have found that true success comes when you pray as if everything depends on a Higher Power while working as if everything depends on you.

Imagine having an ally by your side, a partner with an extraordinary ability to guide and support you. This isn't just any partner; this is an all-knowing, all-loving companion free of limitations. There's no better partner to have on your side as you navigate life's ebbs and flows. We all have different beliefs, and it's important not to judge or criticize other people's beliefs. We are given free agency to choose whom and what we believe in. I salute the Divinity in all people despite our differences.

Often, you might get lost in the maze of life, focusing only on your shortcomings, ensnared by the distractions that surround you. In such moments, you may forget your self-worth, and overlook the unique value you bring to the world. Please don't underestimate how much you would be missed if you weren't here. We are not islands, we are interconnected beings, bound by threads of Love and Friendship.

In our lives, each of us has people who are special to us, and who touch our hearts in profound ways. It's a beautiful two-way connection, a reciprocal dance of Love and Companionship. We are called to extend this love even to those who challenge us, even to our adversaries. It's not an easy task, but it's a worthwhile endeavor.

Each one of you is Special and Unique, blessed with the power to influence others positively in a way that only you can. You have the capacity to uplift, cheer on, and love others through their daily trials and triumphs. This is what makes you special. I believe this gift of being uniquely special helps you to become the best version of yourself.

We are all blessed in countless ways, yet sometimes, though, we're blind to these blessings and unable to see the forest for the trees.

If you find yourself dissatisfied with where you are on your life's journey, remember, you hold the power to change your circumstances. Change starts with a desire, a spark of knowledge that you possess the power to transform your life. As the saying goes, "The journey of a thousand miles begins with a single step." Lao Tzu

Allow me to share with you a roadmap, an eight-step guide that can illuminate your path toward self-transformation.

1. **Visualize Your Best Self:** Close your eyes and imagine the ultimate version of yourself. This is not about physical appearance or material possessions. This is about identifying your core beliefs and self-truths, the ones that make you happy about being who you are. Paint a vivid, detailed picture in your mind. What values does this version of you uphold? How do they interact with the world? Hold onto this image; it's your compass on this journey.

2. **Identify Necessary Changes:** Now that you have a clear vision of your best self, it's time to identify what needs to change in your current situation to align with this vision. These changes might be attitudes, behaviors, relationships, or lifestyle habits. Be honest and brave during this step; it's the foundation for your transformation.

3. **Take Action:** Knowing what needs to change is one thing; taking action is another. Begin implementing these changes in your life. Remember, transformation doesn't happen overnight. It's an evolving process. Even small steps forward are progress.

4. **Commit to Yourself:** Make a pledge to yourself that you will see this journey through, no matter how many obstacles arise. This journey is for you, and the commitment needs to come from within. You are worth the effort and have the power to succeed.

5. **Find an Accountability Partner:** Having someone to share your journey with can be incredibly powerful. Find someone who will hold you accountable, celebrate your victories, and reach out for support when the going gets tough. This person can be a friend, a family member, a mentor, or a coach.

6. **Document Your Journey:** Write down your goals, intentions, and daily tasks. Make sure to set a time limit for your work. Not only does this help keep you organized, but it also serves as a tangible

reminder of your commitment. Plus, there's a unique satisfaction in crossing tasks off the daily to-do list!

7. **Create Beneficial Habits:** Habits are the building blocks of our lives. Replace old, unhelpful habits with new, beneficial ones that align with your vision of your best self. Remember, to create healthy habits, you must be consistent!

8. **Celebrate Your Wins:** Along this journey, take time to celebrate your victories, no matter how small. Each step forward, each positive change, is a victory. These celebrations will fuel your motivation and remind you of your progress.

Always remember, you are Special and Unique, and possess an incredible power within you: the power to transform yourself and help others to do the same. Embrace your journey with love, courage, and steadfast conviction. You have what it takes to become the best version of yourself. Taking the necessary action steps to accomplish your dreams and goals will bring you great Happiness and Satisfaction. Reflecting on quotations always helps to give me additional insight.

Here are a couple of my favorite quotes about being unique:

♥

"In order to be irreplaceable one must always be different."
Coco Chanel.

♥

"What sets you apart can sometimes feel like a burden and it's not. And a lot of time, it's what makes you great."
Emma Stone.

♥

"Most of the time, those people around you that truly love and appreciate you, do so because they find value in your uniqueness; embrace your uniqueness with love."
Dr. Mitch Ergas

♥

"Every lesson in life comes uniquely gift-wrapped and assists you with your uniqueness."
Dr. Mitch Ergas

♥

Chapter Five

A Love Story

In this grand panorama of life, each one of us has had our own brush with love. This emotion, as complex and multi-faceted as it is, paints our memories with hues both bitter and sweet. Today, I wish to share with you a love story that touched my heart deeply, a narrative that intertwines joy and sorrow, hope and despair, love and loss, in a manner so profound that it forever altered the course of my life.

Our tale begins with a young man, a wandering soul whose profession called him to traverse the corners of the world. Often, he found solace in the familiarity of the hotels he frequented, each room a temporary sanctuary amidst his nomadic existence. In one such city, he crossed paths with a radiant young lady who breathed life into the coffee shop where he sought comfort and nourishment during his lunch breaks. As the seasons changed and time ticked away, their casual interactions evolved into a deep friendship, a bond nurtured by shared laughter, stories, and moments that created an oasis of warmth in their otherwise busy lives.

She was a beautiful person with many talents. Her athleticism surpassed that of the young man. Their friendly bouts and competitions became a cherished routine, their camaraderie growing stronger with each game, even though he was rarely victorious.

As the threads of their friendship intertwined, they discovered a deeper connection, a love that bloomed quietly like a flower in the wilderness. However, as destiny would have it, their paths began to diverge. The young man's professional circumstances changed, pulling him away from the city and consequently, from her. She too moved on from the coffee shop, and as if fate was playing a cruel joke, their lines of communication snapped, leaving them adrift in the sea of life.

A year passed by, each day stretching into weeks and months, their connection fading into a distant memory. The young man, however, clung to the hope of reconnecting, like a lifeline. He recalled a fleeting mention of her sister's employment at a local college during one of their conversations. After an arduous search, he managed to contact the sister, who, although hesitant and guarded, provided him with their mother's phone number.

The ensuing months were a test of his perseverance. After numerous failed attempts, he decided to give it one last shot, a final leap of faith. The mother answered, her initial skepticism gradually dissolving as he poured out his heartfelt tale, his longing to reconnect with her daughter. Then, the dam broke. The mother, overcome with emotion, revealed the heart-wrenching truth.

Her daughter, after pulling a grueling double shift, had suffered a fatal accident. She had slipped while reaching for the phone during her shower, hitting her head on the tub and falling unconscious. Her beautiful, long, dark hair blocked the drain, leading to a tragic drowning. Living alone, she was discovered too late, her vibrant life cruelly snuffed out in a split second.

Upon hearing this devastating news, the young man was consumed by a tidal wave of grief. The loss of the love of his dear friend felt like a gaping wound that refused to heal. Amidst the shared tears and shared memories with her mother, he found a glimmer of solace. The mother confided that her daughter often spoke fondly of him and that he was the only man she had ever truly loved.

This revelation, albeit painful, brought a sense of closure to the young man. Their love story had unfolded slowly, like a delicate flower blooming under the gentle warmth of the sun. They had chosen to tread cautiously, cherishing their friendship too much to risk it impulsively. The last time they had been together, they had decided not to escalate their relationship, fearing that it might tarnish their bond.

As she walked away from him that day, with her sweet, loving smile and a final wave etched in his memory, tears began to well up in his eyes as he wondered if he would ever see her again.

The conversation with her mother completed a full circle, bringing a bittersweet sense of healing. He now knew that her feelings mirrored his, that their love was mutual. His heart yearned for what could have been, but amidst the enveloping sorrow, he found a sliver of peace, knowing that their love story, although tragically short, was indeed a tale of mutual affection and respect. The knowledge that they had truly loved each other offered great comfort, a salve to his aching heart.

Love, my dear friends, is an everlasting imprint upon the soul, a memory that time, in all its relentless passage, cannot alter. It's akin to an indelible ink that etches itself upon the canvas of our hearts, forever coloring the way we see and experience the world.

There may come a day when the two souls intertwined in love meet once again in another realm, another universe. The cosmos, in its infinite wisdom, might provide them another chance, another moment to reconnect.

We must always hold onto the hope that love, in all its forms, may transcend the boundaries of time and space.

I wanted to share this story from my own life, a tale that altered the trajectory of my future in ways I never could have anticipated. This narrative, though tinged with sadness, serves as a potent reminder that life is unpredictable and that our plans are but whispers in the wind. It underscores the importance of savoring every moment we're given, of living each day with passion and purpose.

This story, despite its heartbreaking conclusion, remains one of the most poignant chapters of my love life. It was a rollercoaster ride of emotions

- regret, longing, joy, sorrow, and above all, love. The echoes of laughter, the shared dreams of a future that would never be, and the pain of parting - each moment is etched into my heart, a bittersweet symphony of memories that time has failed to dull.

While the physical connection was severed, the spiritual bond endures. The love and friendship we shared, unfettered by conditions or expectations, continue to live on, shaping the contours of my heart and mind. Her memory permeates every fiber of my existence, offering a deeper understanding of what it means to truly love.

As you journey through life, you must remember that love, in all its complexities, is a gift. It's a lesson, a journey, and a memory that time cannot erase. So let yourself love fiercely, live fully, and remember that every ending is but the beginning of another chapter.

I love reflecting on the meanings of others' quotations, as they give me a different perspective about the subject. Love quotations are some of my favorites. Here are some of the ones that have given me hope and inspiration.

♥

"Love is the whole thing, We are only pieces."
Rumi

♥

"And yet I wish but for the thing I have; My
bounty is as boundless as the sea, My love
is deep; the more I give to thee, The more I
have, for both are infinite."
Shakespeare

♥

"Love recognizes no barriers.
Maya Angelou

♥

"If you find someone you love in your life,
then hang onto that love."
Princess Diana

♥

♥

"I love you right up to the moon- and back."
Sam McBratney"

♥

I read somewhere years ago that love
is a memory that time cannot change,
and I totally agree!

♥

:

Chapter Six

Roadblocks to Love

On your journey towards love, you often encounter numerous obstacles that can prevent you from giving and receiving love. I have walked this path and wrestled with these hurdles myself, struggling to fully accept and believe in my worthiness of love. My past: a tapestry woven with threads of trauma, neglect, abuse, and abandonment—had instilled within me a deep-seated negativity of fear and doubt.

I harbored a profound yearning to find someone who would love and accept me for who I truly am. As a free spirit with an entrepreneurial streak, I had always been inclined to chart my own course, to steer my own ship rather than be a passenger on someone else's voyage. This desire led me to explore a diverse array of professions and relationships throughout my life, some met with triumph, others with invaluable lessons.

This same spirit of independence resonated in my quest for love, a journey impeded by five distinct roadblocks that only came to light later in life. These roadblocks served as barriers, preventing me from experiencing and reciprocating love in the authentic, heartfelt manner I aspired to.

Recognizing, understanding, and effectively navigating these roadblocks is crucial for personal growth and development. They have been instrumental in helping to shape my journey. My sincere hope is that they will serve as signposts for you on your path as well.

The Roadblocks to Love

These five roadblocks can indeed be formidable obstacles in your quest for love and fulfillment. But by identifying these barriers and implementing solutions to overcome them, you can start the process of dismantling them; allowing yourself to grow, evolve, and embrace the love you truly deserve.

Roadblock #1 The Shadows of Unresolved Past Experiences

Throughout your life, you encounter a myriad of experiences, some joyous while others traumatic. These experiences, particularly the distressing ones, leave indelible imprints on your psyche and seep into every cell of your being. This trauma, whether consciously remembered or subconsciously repressed, can create both internal and external fortresses.

These fortresses, which are composed of both visible and invisible walls and bridges, serve as protective shields. They are designed to guard you from the anguish of reliving past traumas and the fear of encountering new ones. Yet, this very defense mechanism can become a roadblock, hindering you from fully opening your heart to another soul.

Trauma doesn't merely exist on a psychological level; it permeates your physical and energetic bodies as well. I propose that these imprints are deeply embedded in every layer of your being, with a significant concentration in the seven major and numerous minor energy centers. These centers, often known as chakras, serve as the connection between your physical and subtle bodies, influencing your emotional, mental, and spiritual wellbeing.

A comprehensive understanding of these energy centers will help you grasp how past traumas impact your capacity to love and be loved. You can gain a greater understanding of these energy centers and the role they play in your journey towards healing and self-discovery, by reading about them in a soon to be released digital book by Dr. Ergas titled: Understanding the vital role of your energy centers. By addressing and healing these layered memories, you can begin the process of dismantling the fortress of past traumas, and begin paving the way for a more open, trusting, and loving connection with yourself and others.

Roadblock #2: The Trap of Self-Centeredness

Life, in its beautiful complexity, often pulls you into a whirlpool of personal pursuits and ambitions. Amidst this swirl of aspirations, you may inadvertently become absorbed in your own universe, overlooking the needs and desires of those around you. This self-centered focus, while not inherently negative, becomes problematic when it eclipses your ability to nurture and nourish your relationships, particularly with those you hold dear. While it is important to focus on yourself at the times in your life when self-love and self-confidence are vital to your progression; it's equally important not to be so self-centered that you develop narcissistic behavior and ignore everyone around you.

Recognizing this tunnel vision is the first step towards transformation. It calls for a mirror to your soul, an honest introspection that lays bare your behaviors and patterns. Once you acknowledge this self-absorption, you can begin to recalibrate your actions and attitudes, shifting your focus from 'I' to 'We'. Sometimes professional help is needed to work through this behavior.

One of the most potent antidotes to self-centeredness is service to others. By directing your attention and energy towards the welfare of others, you are able to transcend your individualistic bubble. In the act of giving, you receive - a paradox that holds profound truth. As you lose yourself in the service of others, you discover facets of your being that lay dormant, unveiling a richer, deeper sense of self. This isn't merely a philosophical concept; it's a divine principle that breathes life into your existence.

Yet, it's essential to strike a balance. While service to others is transformative, it should not come at the cost of self and family. The wellspring of love within you must be replenished regularly. After all, you cannot pour from an empty vessel. Self-love isn't a luxury; it's a necessity. However, like all good things, it requires moderation. An excessive focus on self-love can veer into self-centeredness, leading to the neglect of your loved ones.

Thus, you find yourself walking a delicate tightrope, balancing self-love with service to others. When navigated with wisdom and mindfulness, this journey can lead you to a more fulfilled, love-infused life. One of the things that has helped me with this balancing process is, by Praying and Meditating for Divine guidance daily; and then following the counsel I receive.

Roadblock #3: The Enigma of Communication Challenges

As I journeyed through the winding paths of my life, I came to understand that effective communication is the cornerstone of any good relationship. This revelation, gleaned from personal experiences and countless interactions, holds a profound significance that cannot be overstated.

Many years ago, I chanced upon a book entitled "Men are from Mars, Women are from Venus" by John Gray. This insightful work unraveled the intricate tapestry of gender-based communication differences. It was a revelation, an unveiling of the unique wiring of men and women, and their distinct ways of processing information and emotions. I wholeheartedly recommend this book to anyone who wishes to better understand these fascinating differences.

Over time, I have witnessed firsthand the impact of these differences. Left unrecognized and unvalidated, they can sow seeds of discord, fuel arguments, and breed rejection between partners. The constant stress associated with these communication challenges can manifest physically and emotionally, leading to health disorders, marital discord, overall family dysfunction, and divorce.

Yet, within these challenges lie opportunities for growth and understanding. By working through our communication issues, we learn to respect each other's perspectives, embrace our imperfections, and celebrate our differences.

In my life, a significant source of healing has been my wife, a remarkable Psychotherapist and Counselor. Her wisdom and insights have enriched my understanding of effective communication. I've seen the transformative power of her sincere and honest guidance with our children, family members, and even strangers. Her chosen career success speaks volumes about her ability to help others navigate their path to recovery.

In essence, communication is a dance, a delicate interplay of speaking and listening. It requires patience, understanding, and respect for our differences. By mastering this dance, we can foster stronger and more fulfilling relationships that can stand the test of time.

Roadblock #4: The Struggle to Apologize and Forgive

There's a profound yet challenging aspect of human interaction - the ability to apologize when necessary and the ability to accept one when necessary. This seesaw of humility and forgiveness is often obstructed by a towering wall of ego.

I recall a poignant tale of a dear friend, a tragic narrative that underscores this struggle. This friend, in a moment of uncontrolled anger, deeply wounded his family. Despite his wrongdoing, his stubborn pride prevented him from admitting his fault and seeking forgiveness. His family, willing to forgive but awaiting an apology, gradually distanced themselves.

As years turned into decades, his parents fell ill and passed away. His remaining siblings - a brother and sister - reached out repeatedly, hoping for reconciliation and closure. Yet, he remained ensnared in his web of guilt, shame, fear, and bitterness. Even when tragedy struck again, claiming the life of his beloved younger brother, he remained silent.

Years later, in a desperate attempt to mend the broken threads of familial bond, he reached out to his remaining sister. To his despair, he learned that she had succumbed to breast cancer. He was left alone, haunted by the ghosts of lost opportunities for closure, and burdened with a grief that was intensified by regret.

As time passed, his sorrow transformed into bitterness, anger, and resentment. He blamed his family for the fallout, ignoring his role in it. His emotional turmoil manifested physically as debilitating arthritis. He lived out his days in solitude and pain, a grim testament to the destructive power of withheld apologies and unaccepted forgiveness.

His story serves as a stark reminder of the healing power of apology and forgiveness. These seemingly simple acts unlock the heart, allowing love to flow freely, and foster understanding and compassion. By making amends, we initiate a healing process for ourselves and everyone involved.

The journey towards forgiveness and reconciliation can seem like a daunting task, akin to a thousand-mile trek. Yet, as Lao Tzu wisely said, "The journey of a thousand miles begins with a single step." Sometimes, it falls upon us to take that first step. If the other party isn't receptive, we must exercise patience and understanding. We can only do our part; the rest, we must surrender to a higher power.

In essence, the act of apologizing and accepting forgiveness is a testament to our humanity. It is an affirmation of our capacity for love and understanding, a beacon of hope in our shared journey of growth and healing..

Roadblock #5: Negative Repetitive Patterns

'These patterns have been referred to as cognitive/emotional loops or repeating patterns. Here your thoughts and beliefs make you think that the story you are telling yourself, is real. This is based on the feelings you have at the time of the repeated pattern; which makes the process more intense." Ex: Pouring gas onto a fire, leading to expended energy which slows you down and prevents you from moving forward. I have added some of my thoughts to the material pertaining to Letting go of negative repetitive patterns, with the rest of the material on Negative Repetitive Patterns coming from the ACA/WHO's books. More details about these patterns and their possible solutions are given in Chapter 8 of this book. The ACA/WHO's book and workbook titles are given along with their contact link for a more in depth study of their program.

Here are just a few examples:

- You have to be right all the time
- You have to be the center of attention
- You are a know it all
- You are easily distracted
- You have negative behaviors and thoughts
- You would rather snack than eat healthy
- You hate your bad habits, but can't change them

Here are some possible solutions:

- Meditation and prayer to receive insight on how you can make changes
- Create the right mindset and practice it daily
- Accountability partners like support groups for people doing the work
- Focus exercises like yoga, pilates, tai chi/energy, crosswords, journaling

- Celebrating your accomplishments
- Don't beat yourself up, keep moving forward and never give up
- Implement time management to keep you from distractions
- Create a list and check it off as you complete it daily
- Do things differently than you have been
- Only surround yourself with positive people
- Commit to the process of change
- Create new habits to replace the old ones.
- Get professional help from Counselors, Coaches, Energy Healers, etc.

The Path to Love's Enlightenment

As you journey through life, you will inevitably confront these roadblocks on the path to love. These obstacles, as daunting as they may initially appear, are powerful teachers in disguise. They enlighten you about your inner self and the profound essence of love.

Love, in its truest sense, is a harmonious blend of vulnerability, generosity, understanding, forgiveness, and above all, growth. It calls upon us to bravely expose our hearts, to give without expecting anything in return, to strive for understanding rather than to be understood, to forgive unconditionally, and to constantly evolve. Confronting these facets of love often presents us with hurdles that test our emotional resilience and determination.

Identifying these roadblocks is the first step towards a transformative journey. By doing so, you begin to understand the intricate emotional map of your heart, the depth of your capacity for love and the strength within you to overcome adversity. Thus, you empower yourself to experience and reciprocate love in its most genuine, heartfelt form. I have often used the answers I got from my reflection exercises to help better understand these 5 roadblocks that interfered with my capacity to Love more deeply.

Reflection Exercise: Find a peaceful place where you can sit undisturbed. Close your eyes, take three deep, calming breaths, and allow tranquility to envelop you. Now, bring to mind one of the roadblocks you faced on your journey of love. What emotions does it stir within you? How did you navigate this hurdle? What valuable lessons did it impart?

Once you've pondered these questions, visualize yourself surmounting this roadblock. Use the answers that you receive from the questions, to help you with solutions that are unique to you. Imagine the courage, wisdom, and empathy required to conquer it. Feel the surge of accomplishment, liberation, and personal growth that comes with each resolution.

Reflection Questions:

1. What roadblocks have you encountered on your personal journey of love?

2. How have these roadblocks shaped your relationships and your perception of love?

3. What strategies did you employ to overcome these roadblocks? Which tactics were effective and which ones fell short?

4. What insights did you glean from these experiences?

5. How can they help you with your personal growth and understanding of love?

6. How can you apply these lessons to future roadblocks and other challenges in your relationships?

Bonus: The P.O.E. Technique

This technique is best utilized when you need to change your mood quickly. I like to say it helps to elevate you away from the "Stinkin Thinkin" into a higher, more positive frame of mind. That's why I put it at the end of the Roadblocks Chapter, as it's more of a temporary way to rise above the roadblock until you can do the necessary work to completely move beyond it permanently. It's not what happens to you that matters, it's how you handle it that makes all the difference. When you begin anything, the first and most important step is to have the right mindset. I believe if you can see it and believe it, you can achieve it.

It came to me on one of the darkest days of my life. I was severely depressed having gone through a short marriage and quick divorce in which my baby son Mikey would no longer be living in the same state with me. I grieved the loss of him not being around me, and on top of that, I was working and going to school full time. The financial pressure to pay bills and child support on two children was tough at the time. Wanting to be the best Dad possible for my daughter Ereca weighed heavy on me as her mother and I were no longer friends. I did not get to spend as much time with her or my son and was grieving badly. I was barely scraping by, and almost homeless at one point. One day I hit rock bottom, I found myself lying on the floor, exhausted, feeling unwanted and unloved, with thoughts of suicide running through my head; literally at the end of my rope. With tears in my eyes, I called my daughter Ereca to say goodbye. She answered the phone and we began talking. It was the love and compassion she showed me that kept me from making a serious mistake. After talking for a while, and me assuring her that I was okay; we got off the phone. I immediately began praying for Divine Guidance for my life.

After a few minutes, a couple of questions popped into my head.

1. The first question was: Is what you are thinking about right now, Positive or Negative?

2. The second question was: How does what you are thinking about right now make you feel?

3. The third thing that came to me was the process, how to use the information that I received.

I was told to first identify whether or not what I was thinking was positive or negative? If I said it was positive, then I was instructed to enjoy the thought process, as no changes were necessary. If it was negative, I was instructed to ask myself the question, how does it make you feel? I responded-that it made me feel sad. Then I was instructed to think about a time in my life when I was at my happiest, or a special event that made me happy; and to reflect upon it until I began feeling the energy of the experience bring me up. If that didn't work fast enough for me, I was instructed to begin counting my blessings, all the things in my life that I was thankful for; my children, my health, a job, friends, family, pets, a place to live, a car to drive, freedoms, talents, food, etc. You get the picture!

I was amazed at how this technique helped me back then and still does today. It helps me to get from a negative space to a positive one quickly allowing me to function properly when I need to be on. I have shared this technique with many of my family, friends, and patients who all say that it has helped them tremendously. The moment in time when you raise your energy vibration from a negative mindset to a positive one, and you feel the negative emotions shifting into positive ones, is known as The Point of Empowerment because you are quickly empowered at that moment in time. This technique will not work for deep-seated trauma, I recommend professional help for it; Psychotherapy, Counseling, and Energetic Therapeutics work best for that type. I have used the P.O.E. technique for issues like anxiety, fear, sadness, depression, and anger; with great results. Remember, when you find yourself in a bad situation; stop and begin the two-step process of identifying the type of thought and how it's making you feel. Then follow the changing process. After you have done this enough times it happens automatically without you having to go through the steps. I tell everyone that this technique is like anything else, it works for some people, and for others it isn't enough. I find the more often you use it, the better it works for you when you need it. Enjoy the process! Dr. Mitch Ergas.

The Philosopher Rumi said that: "Your task is not to seek for love, but merely to seek and find all the barriers within yourself that you have built against it."

Remember, each person's journey of love is unique, a tapestry woven from their individual experiences. Sometimes we resist love because of the pain of having been hurt, and not wanting to experience the pain again. The roadblocks we face are opportunities for introspection and growth. By learning to navigate them, we cultivate resilience, compassion, and understanding, enabling us to experience and express love in its most authentic, heartfelt form.

And as I always say, if you try and are not getting the results you want, reach out to a professional who can assist you on your healing path. Everybody can use a little help when it comes to overcoming the Roadblocks to Love. Therapists, Counselors, Coaches, and Energy Healers can guide you and make the process a lot easier.

Chapter Seven

The Power
of Forgiveness

There exists an often overlooked yet profoundly transformative power - the power of forgiveness. I covered most of the material about it in earlier chapters, but due to its importance; I wanted to share another story with you that demonstrates the power of change it provides. This divine force has the potential to liberate our spirits from the shackles of resentment that can breed illness and imbalance within us. It is a healing balm that soothes the wounds of our hearts and restores our inner equilibrium.

It is about acknowledging our human imperfections and creating space for compassion and understanding.

In my own life, I've found that embracing forgiveness is akin to bathing in a refreshing stream of grace. It washes away the stains of past mistakes and offers us the opportunity to start anew. This divine principle can propel us forward, and help us to reach the twilight of our lives; without the regrets and remorse of not reconciling with those dear to us-our family, our friends, and our loved ones.

As you delve into this story, I invite you to open your heart and mind to the emotions that you experience. Let the narrative take you on a journey, prompting self-reflection and inspiring you to embrace the healing essence of forgiveness in your own life.

I was once blessed to cross paths with a woman in her middle years who sought my guidance for Energy Healing. Her body had become a battlefield, marred by arthritis and a host of other ailments. A dear friend introduced us, and I'll admit, our first meeting stirred a sense of trepidation within me due to her esteemed professional standing in a field I believed she knew more intimately than I.

As we journeyed together over a period of several weeks, a delicate connection began to form between us. In the safe harbor of this bond, she unveiled a deep-seated secret, a story of recurrent sexual abuse that had cast a dark shadow over her childhood and seeped into her teenage years. Despite mustering the courage to share her painful truth with her mother and aunt, they dismissed her experiences as fabrications. The moment she could, she broke free from that house, leaving behind the echoes of her torment.

She shared how she had navigated the intricate maze of various therapeutic modalities, seeking solace from her mental burdens. Yet, the haunting specters of her past continued to linger. In a final bid for liberation, she decided to venture into the realm of energy healing, hoping to finally; get rid of the demons of her past.

After several months of walking this path together, we began to see the first signs of progress. She was gradually opening up to the healing process, a crucial step to her journey towards inner peace.

During one of our sessions, she revealed that her abuser, now a fragile man in his eighties, was in the twilight of his life; living out his remaining days in an assisted living facility. Guided by my spiritual intuition, I felt that she had very little time to accomplish this task. I suggested that she seek a way to let go of the shame and feelings of resentment she held before he departed. Closure, I believe, is a vital part of healing. I understand that this advice might not resonate or be applicable in every case of abuse, but when guided by Divine wisdom, it can lead to profound healing.

Her reaction to my suggestion was a storm of anger, an emotion I understood and empathized with. I gently encouraged her to seek her own spiritual guidance and see if it would echo the path I had suggested.

After a silence that stretched over weeks, she reached out to schedule another session. I welcomed her back with open arms, relieved to hear from her. She apologized for her previous anger and shared, through a veil of tears, that her prayers had confirmed my guidance.

The thought of confronting her abuser filled her with fear. But empowered by her own spiritual confirmation, she decided to follow through. We agreed that her best friend would accompany her for moral support and that they would meet in the serene garden of his assisted living facility, a peaceful sanctuary adorned with blooming flowers and sheltering shade trees.

As the frail, white-haired man approached, she felt a wave of fear and triggered memories well-up within her. However, at that very moment; she used The Point of Empowerment Technique she had previously learned and was able to regain control over her emotions.

Their conversation began with mundane pleasantries, during which she discovered his excitement at having a family member visit. When she finally summoned the courage to speak about forgiveness, he interrupted her. With tears welling up in his eyes, he said, "You have no need to apologize for anything, you have done nothing wrong. I cannot remember hardly anything from my past, but, if I have ever hurt you in any way, I am truly sorry, please forgive me."

This moment sparked a surge of emotions within her-a catharsis of sorts. She realized that this humbled, old man, now lost in the fog of dementia, could no longer harm her. She felt the sincerity of his apology resonate through her entire being, and the weight of the trauma was lifted; finally giving her the closure she had been yearning for.

They spent some more time with the man, and as they prepared to leave, she felt a newfound compassion and sadness for him. She had walked the path of true forgiveness, recognizing his obliviousness to his past actions. Her forgiveness blossomed into unconditional love, as they reveled in the present moment, unhindered by the past.

This poignant experience brings to mind a biblical verse, "Where two or more are gathered together in my name, there I will be also." In the act of forgiveness, she discovered not just closure, but the divine presence guiding her towards healing and inner peace.

In our next meeting, she poured out the details of their encounter to me. Tears of joy cascaded down her cheeks as she recounted the serendipitous closure she was able to find with this relative. As fate would have it, he passed away a mere two weeks after their healing moments together. She expressed profound gratitude for having listened to the insight we both received, and for my words of encouragement. I congratulated her for taking the brave action steps she took towards her healing process.

As time unfurled, I watched an extraordinary transformation unfold in her. Her arthritis and other physical afflictions began to recede, as if they were shadows chased away by the dawn of her newfound peace. The changes in her physical body were palpable - a testament to the profound impact of long-held stress on our health, and the body's ability to heal itself! Today, she radiates a vitality that belies her age, looking and feeling a decade younger than her chronological years.

I gently reminded her that by surrendering his karmic debt to a higher power, she had relinquished the burden of dealing with it. I assured her that in the grand scheme of the universe, justice prevails, and each one of us must bear the consequences of our actions toward others.

Today, she stands tall as a beacon of happiness, health, and success. She made the conscious choice not to dwell in the past but to live fully in the present. In many cases, it is not possible to confront those that have abused us, so we have to release the trauma to our Higher Power and continue to do our healing work. Sometimes the best we can do is to learn how to manage the pain until we heal. When it is possible to have this type of a healing experience; the power of forgiveness is indeed invaluable. It sweeps away the debris of negative emotions, replacing them with the healing balm of love. It kindles a spark of hope within us, propelling us forward on our life's journey.

Forgiveness is the soothing balm that heals us, propelling us forward, and it opens our hearts to love more profoundly and live with a greater sense of richness in our lives. I've voiced this truth before, yet it's so essential that it warrants repeating: love and forgiveness are inseparable companions on our life's journey. Love paves the way for forgiveness, and through the act of forgiving, we encounter the most profound expression of love. This beautiful dance between love and forgiveness is a cornerstone in our pursuit of a fulfilled life.

The conscious application of this principle is pivotal for our personal growth. One of the tools that helped me to better understand the benefits of forgiveness was through the questions I created below. I reflected on the emotions they elicited in me and connected to the benefits of the answers that were revealed. This is a personal journey for each of us, enjoy the process, learn from your answers, and be open and receptive to both forgiving others and being forgiven yourself.

Take a moment, a quiet, reflective pause, as you ask and answer these 7 questions:

1. How did you feel when you were forgiven by someone else?

2. How did you feel when you forgave someone else?

3. How did you feel when you asked for forgiveness, and were turned down?

4. How did you feel when you refused to forgive someone else?

5. Where in your life can you summon the strength of forgiveness, to free yourself from the shadows of past hurts or regrets?

6. How can you nurture a deeper reservoir of love in your life, and

how might this nourish your capacity to forgive?

7. When you think of forgiveness, what's the first thing that comes to your mind?

Now is the time to tap into the transformative power of forgiveness and love. By doing so, you can liberate yourself from the constraints of your past, mend your emotional wounds, and navigate towards living your most authentic life. The journey may be filled with challenges, but remember, every step taken in love and forgiveness brings you closer to a brighter, more fulfilling future. True freedom lies in your ability to be the forgiveness and love you seek. Dr. Ergas!

Chapter Eight

Family Creating Love's Blueprint

(For Better or Worse)

Family, the primal and most potent influence in our lives, leaves imprints upon our souls from our earliest recollections to our present existence. These impressions, a blend of brightness and shadow, resonate deeply within my own personal journey.

In my youth, I vividly remember threads of wisdom that were profoundly enriching. Yet, they were interwoven with numerous strands of experiences that were to understate, less than wholesome. These instances, marred by dysfunction, have etched indelible marks on my psyche.

My childhood was framed in an era where mothers were depicted as nurturing beings and fathers as breadwinners. My reality, however, painted a starkly contrasting picture. My father, ensnared in the throes of a gambling addiction, deserted us. My mother, perpetually battling for survival, was left to provide for six children armed only with an eighth-grade education. In such circumstances, emotional sustenance and tenderness were luxuries we could scarcely afford.

I recall moments of yearning for my mother's soothing embrace when illness struck, awaiting her return home with bated breath. Instead, I was met with her aloof, distant demeanor. The nurturing I yearned for and desperately needed was absent, not because of indifference but because she was stretched thin by the burdens of providing for our family. Moreover, her own upbringing was fraught with hardships. As painful as these memories are, I now, as a 70-year old man, reflect upon them with empathy for my mother. She was herself a shattered soul - how could I have expected her to offer me something she herself had never been given?

Despite the void left by my mother's inability to express love and my father's complete abandonment, my siblings emerged as beacons of hope in my life. I often found solace in daydreams, envisioning a different life born into a family adorned with wealth, fame, or professional success. Yet, when my thoughts drift back to the reality of my brothers and sisters, my heart surges with gratitude. Each one has significantly shaped my identity in their own unique way. Through our bonds, I have been given the chance to learn, to mature, and to transform.

My bond with my older brother Nick was the strongest. With barely 18 months between us, he was my rock and protector. Despite his tough exterior, he had a soft, teddy bear-like side that was visible only to those who were closest to him. Over the years, we maintained our connection, talking often even though we lived in different states. He had a zest for life, a great sense of humor, and an innate ability to aid people on their journeys.

We shared a love for card games, especially hearts. We made an invincible team, always knowing how to play our hands together without uttering a single word. Our silent communication often frustrated our opponents, but it was a testament to our unspoken bond.

Nick was not even 18 when he left for the Vietnam War. I was a junior in high school then, and my memories from that time are somewhat hazy now. However, I distinctly remember the constant worry that gnawed at me. My best friend, my father-figure, was fighting in a war that was mired in controversy, and I lived in perpetual fear of him not returning home; while trying to have faith that he would.

This chapter of my life unfurled a rapid succession of profound lessons in avoidant attachment. The ties that bound me to my family, which should have been threads of love and connection, were instead steeped in the bitterness of pain and echoes of our dysfunctional existence. The paradox, as eloquently elucidated by Brene Brown in her thought-provoking book "The Gifts of Imperfection," lies in the fact that we, as humans, are hardwired for connection.

That's why, despite the formidable obstacles, I dedicated years of my life to reconfiguring my innate patterns of love and connection, acutely aware that my early familial influences had primed me for failure in many ways.

Over time, I sought solace and understanding in the counsel of various forms of therapy. However, the empathetic resonance and comprehension I yearned for eluded me, leaving my desired outcomes unfulfilled. In hindsight, it was likely my unreadiness to revisit and relive the traumas of my past that impeded my progress. I have since come to understand that we often bury our traumas deep within us to avoid facing them head-on, only for them to resurface persistently, clamoring for healing.

A friend once asked me, "Why do I keep attracting the same type of men into my life?"

I explained that she was pulling similar individuals towards her repeatedly because there were lessons that both parties needed to learn to advance. I firmly believe that when lessons lie ahead of you, the Universe invariably presents you with the opportunities to learn them. Life, in my perspective, is an ever-evolving process. When you remain open and receptive to the challenges that life throws your way, you can experience them, learn from them, and subsequently move beyond them. On the road to self-mastery, the enlightenment and wisdom you glean from your trials illuminate your path to the next lesson. Once you master or complete a lesson, its repetition becomes unnecessary.

It was around this time, I remember having a conversation with Sebastian, a friend of mine from College; about meeting a therapist he worked with named Catherine. He felt like the two of us would hit it off. I was resistant at first and he was very persistent, so we agreed to meet at a Vegetarian restaurant called Harmony. He wanted to make sure that

I showed up, so he agreed to drive. Little did I know at the time, she had only agreed to meet with me if he came. Also, she would not allow him to give me her phone number until she met and approved of me. After our meeting and dinner, we both had a strange feeling of destiny, and she even wrote in her journal four days later: "I think he knows what I know." And she was right. Although outwardly we came from very different worlds, our connection has helped us both to learn and grow in ways we could never have imagined. She had Master's degrees in both Psychology and Counseling at the time and has since devoted nearly 30 years to helping countless people on their healing journeys. Catherine illuminated the intricacies of family dynamics, their influences, and their impact on my life. She introduced me to the transformative concept of "Nourishing Our Souls" and elucidated the profound potential of connection when we commit to doing this healing work.

Journeying through life with her I have learned a variety of ways to nourish my soul. You will learn some of the ways that you can nourish your soul in the next Chapter.

Breaking free from the shadows of childhood traumas, whether they're mental, physical, emotional, or sexual, can be an uphill battle. It often requires professional help and a strong will to change. But, believe me when I say this, it's a battle worth fighting. If you don't confront these traumas, you risk being trapped in the past and held back by the negative influences that isolate you from others.

We are all social beings, born with an innate need for connection. Positive influences foster this connection, bringing with it a sense of belonging, joy, and love. Yet, navigating family functions can sometimes be like walking through a minefield of triggers, reminding you of those negative influences that have shaped your life.

I know it's hard when your family laughs off things that deeply affect you, unaware or indifferent to the fact that we all process things differently. What might seem trivial to them could awaken dormant traumas from your past.

I came to realize that many influences from my family during my formative years were not serving me well. They were harmful not only to me but also to those around me. So, I embarked on a journey of self-discovery and healing. I work to let go of the unhealthy influences, replacing them with healthier, more positive ones. An effort I might add that's not for the faint of heart, yet can be very rewarding.

And so can you my friends if you are willing to put in the work. I believe it's never too late to change the narrative of your life, to turn the page and start a new chapter. Someone once said, "Families are Forever." If this is true, healing your family wounds should be one of your top priorities. Remember, you have the power within you to rewrite your own story. As you are the one who writes your own story, you decide the person you will become. We are all unique in that what works for one, might not work for another. To create a new blueprint for yourself, you must first look at your old blueprint. Some of the things you learn from your early childhood years are disempowering to you and can lead to a dysfunctional life in adulthood.

Let's explore some of the old blueprint issues and ways to create a new healthier one. My wife introduced me to two excellent resources available to help you better understand your early blueprint and how to change it: The Loving Parent Guidebook & the Twelve Steps of Adult Children: Steps Workbook. Both of these workbooks are available through the Adult Children of Alcoholics® & Dysfunctional Families World Service Organization on their website https://adultchildren.org//

I will share some of the basic challenges and solutions that are offered in these books. For a more in depth study, I highly recommend reading and applying the lessons found in them. I believe you can benefit greatly by doing so. I am not an affiliate, partner, etc. and do not receive any profits from any of the sources that I mention. I just feel that they contain powerful insights and tools for healing.

Tony A. was credited with creating what is known as ACA's "Laundry List" of character traits Adult Children of Alcoholics® & Other Dysfunctional Families often share. You may recognize some of these traits in your Old Blueprint challenges: These are developed from the many interactions with your family members during your childhood.

- Mistrust
- Procrastination
- Perfectionism
- Isolation
- Self-Centeredness

As you do the work and evolve in your healing journey, both you and your family can experience healing. Here are some of the benefits you may experience more of:

- Trust
- Self-Love
- Emotional Sobriety
- Maturity
- Joy
- Ability to be of Service
- Friendship

Quotations have often helped me to reflect and see the importance of families. I believe they can benefit you as well.

Here are a few of the quotes that have inspired and motivated me when dealing with family issues. They remind me of the importance of my family for better or worse. Notice what you feel when you read them, and reflect upon the importance of the message. Do you get inspired and motivated as you read and reflect? By embracing and understanding your old Blueprint, you can begin to create a new one for yourself.

❤

"When everything goes to hell, the people who stand by you without flinching-they are your family."
Jim Butcher

❤

"The love of a family is a life's greatest blessing."
Eva Burrows.

❤

"Family is not an important thing, it's everything."
Michael J. Fox

❤

"Family is the one vehicle in our lives that helps us to learn more about ourselves than we could ever learn on our own."
Dr. Mitch Ergas

❤

Chapter Nine

Nourishing
the Soul

For a considerable span of my life, I have embarked on a profound inward journey, meticulously deciphering the intricate blueprint of love and connection that forms an integral part of my being. The endeavor to craft my own family as an adult, using this initial blueprint as a foundation, has proven to be a formidable challenge.

Indeed, it wasn't until my most recent journey back into the institution of marriage and family that I was serendipitously guided towards tying the knot with a therapist. This fortuitous turn of events has been nothing short of transformative.

My life partner, who I spoke about in an earlier chapter; has been my steadfast companion for over a quarter of a century. She has enriched my understanding of human relationships and self-improvement. She also imparted to me the invaluable wisdom, that reaching out to others for guidance is not a sign of weakness, but an act of courage and self-care. This becomes particularly significant when one finds themselves stuck in a rut, unable to break free from the chains of stagnation to move forward in life.

She has shed light on the transformative power of change, emphasizing its potential to heal wounds inflicted by past traumas. These invisible scars often imprison us within our own hearts and minds, preventing us from experiencing the joy and fulfillment that life has to offer.

The healing process necessitates a conscious effort to make changes, no matter how small or seemingly insignificant they may appear. Each step taken towards healing is a step away from the shackles of the past, paving the way for a happier, healthier future.

Through her wisdom, I have learned that we are not destined to remain captive to our past traumas. With courage, resilience, and the right guidance, we can rewrite our blueprints and construct a life that resonates with love, connection, and personal fulfillment.

Drawing upon the wisdom of renowned trauma expert Dr. Gabor Mate, who astutely observed, "Our need for attachment often collides with our need for authenticity," Catherine opened up to the profound resonance this insight had in her life.

As she navigated through the early influences of her family, she found herself on a quest to discover and understand her authentic self. Maybe some of us can relate?

She noted, "I frequently found myself attempting to conform to the norms of groups that were vastly different from me. I was constantly trying to discern what behavior was acceptable and what was not. In a world so richly diverse, I often felt a sense of indifference from people, which further triggered my early childhood traumas and deprived me of the emotional nourishment necessary for my survival."

While embarking on a transformative journey of healing, Catherine discovered and developed the guided imagery cd mentioned in this book. Working in the world of Dual Diagnosis, Addiction Treatment and Trauma Recovery introduced her to the recovery principle of "Let go and Let God."

In a moment of desperation, seeking solace and relief from her challenges, she retreated into her tiny closet to perform a version of this guided imagery exercise. Little did she know that this moment would serve as a spiritual turning point, forever altering the trajectory of her life. The transformation she experienced was so profound that she felt compelled to share it with therapy groups, hoping others could reap the benefits she had.

For eight long years, countless individuals praised the effectiveness of Catherine's method, constantly inquiring if they could find a recorded version of it. Despite the overwhelming success and demand for her practice, Catherine hesitated to record it, believing at the time that the obstacles were too numerous to overcome. However, after eight years of reluctance, she finally decided to open herself up to unseen possibilities.

It was then that the Universe conspired to bring her angels in human form who played their crucial roles in recording and producing her transformative guided imagery. Despite being produced using 2009 technologies, "Nourishing Your Soul: A Guided Imagery for Letting Go" has been instrumental in fostering calmness, centeredness, and relaxation within me and many others while navigating the turbulent times in our lives. It continues to be a potent tool for countless individuals on their healing journeys. It stands as a testament to Catherine's resilience and her unwavering dedication to helping others navigate the complexities of life. Soon, this powerful process will be even more widely available with the release of her forthcoming book, Nourishing Your Soul.

As I engaged with Catherine and began to comprehend more about my own past, I realized the crucial importance of releasing its hold over me.

The most transformative realization came when I embraced those life events and experiences that have served to nourish my soul. My fervent hope for everyone is that you too can identify and embrace those things that feed your soul. This, I believe, is one of the most significant acts of self-love you can perform, with far-reaching benefits for both yourself and those around you.

8 Ways to Nourish Your Soul

Throughout my journey, I've discovered that the process of nourishing one's soul and fostering the capacity to let go is profoundly amplified when you consciously immerse yourself in the present moment, truly embracing its inherent beauty. Here are 8 practices that have served as invaluable tools for soul nourishment throughout my personal journey:

1. **Journaling:** There's a certain magic that unfolds when pen meets paper. Journaling provides a sanctuary for your thoughts and emotions, a safe haven where you can unravel your deepest fears and highest hopes. It serves as a mirror to your soul, reflecting your innermost thoughts and feelings back to you, enabling you to understand them better. Over time, this practice can help you identify patterns, triggers, and ways to better navigate your life's journey.

2. **Watching the Sunrise/Sunset:** The simple act of observing the sunrise or sunset can be deeply meditative. As the sky paints itself in hues of orange, pink, and gold, one cannot help but feel a sense of awe and wonder. It's a gentle reminder of life's cyclical nature - no matter how dark the night, the sun will always rise again. This daily spectacle encourages introspection, renewal, and a deeper appreciation for the transient beauty of life.

3. **Being of Service:** There's an unparalleled joy that stems from acts of service. Whether it's lending a helping hand to a stranger or contributing to a cause close to your heart, service transcends the self and connects us to the larger human family. It fosters empathy, compassion, and a sense of fulfillment that far surpasses materialistic pleasure. This reminds me of a Bible verse. Let me paraphrase- "When you have done it unto the least of these my brethren; you have done it unto me." Jesus

4. **Listening to Music:** The universal language of music has the power to touch souls and stir emotions like nothing else can. Whether it's a melody that makes your heart soar or lyrics that resonate with your current state of mind, music offers comfort, inspiration, and a sense of connection. For me, music touches me in ways that nothing else does. Just like the messages in this book, Billy Joel's new song; "Turn The Lights Back On" is a

reflection about the importance of love and forgiveness and the power of never giving up.

5. **Meditation:** Meditation is a journey inward, a practice that helps quiet the noise of the outside world and helps you tune into your inner voice. It fosters clarity, peace, and a deeper understanding of ourselves. Over time, consistent meditation can help you respond rather than react to life's challenges, enhancing your overall well-being. There are many different techniques out there- Transcendental Meditation, etc. Find the one that resonates with you and practice it regularly for best results.

6. **Prayer:** Regardless of one's religious or spiritual beliefs, prayer can be a powerful tool for seeking solace and guidance. It serves as a lifeline to a Higher Power, a way to surrender your fear and anxiety, and help you gain strength and wisdom. Prayer can bring a profound sense of peace and purpose, an anchor during life's storms.

7. **Practicing Gratitude:** Cultivating an attitude of gratitude can transform your perception of life. By appreciating the blessings that are often taken for granted - like your health, friends, family, the gift of life, and the love you receive - you cultivate a mindset of abundance. This practice enhances positivity, enriches your relationships, and increases your overall sense of happiness and well-being.

8. **Connecting with a Higher Power:** This connection transcends the physical world and touches the realm of the spiritual. It offers a broader perspective on life, and helps you to understand that you are part of something much larger than yourself. This realization can instill a deep sense of faith and resilience, guiding you through life's ups and downs.

I invite you to select one or two of these practices and incorporate them into your daily routine. Pay attention to how they influence your feelings and overall state of being. Document your observations, noting which practices resonate most deeply with you and fuel your spirit. Then you can keep going until you have implemented all eight. This journey of self-discovery is personal and unique, so take your time and savor each step along the path.

❤

"Every challenge in life, helps to nourish your soul and brings you one step closer to your destiny."
Dr. Mitch Ergas

❤

Chapter Ten

What's Love Got to Do with It?

(Everything)

When I was young, I would listen to people talk about love like it was a magic wand. My grandmother, in particular, taught us that positive thoughts and love could bring about miraculous healing for those who believed in the power of them.

This concept was scary at times.

There were people in my life who professed their love one minute and then would beat, curse, or emotionally abuse you in another.

As a child, this was confusing.

Their actions did not match their words.

Love for me was a double-edged sword: do as I say and I will love you, but if you don't do what I say, I will beat you, abuse you, or abandon you.

Is it any wonder why some people who are abused grow up to treat others in the same way that they were treated?

If these people don't do the work of healing their own wounds, they often inflict the same type of pain onto others, even though that may not be their intention. Thankfully, I did not continue the cycle of abuse I endured. I just carried it buried deep inside of me until I was capable of facing and releasing it.

I acknowledge that not every household is a mirror image of mine, which was a cauldron of dysfunctionality. The words "I love you" rarely escaped my parents' lips. If they ever did, the memory was swiftly erased by the fear of impending violence that cast a long, dark shadow over our everyday existence. In our home, disobedience was not tolerated. It was met with harsh reprimands or physical punishment.

Growing up, my siblings and I endured various forms of abuse—mental, physical, emotional, and, for some, sexual. Amidst the turmoil, it was difficult to truly hear or understand what was being said. Our bodies were perpetually on high alert for the next potential threat. This constant state of fight or flight wreaked havoc on our health, and affected each of us differently. We tried to cope the best we could. Looking back, I now realize that the occasional moments of tranquility were invaluable gifts, providing us with temporary relief for our overwrought nervous systems.

Despite the chaos, my siblings and I managed to carve out pockets of fun and peace. I remember sitting under the shade of an orange tree as the sun beat down all around me. I can still feel the warmth of the white sand on my feet, taste the sweetness of the orange juice on my tongue, and smell the invigorating orange scent from the oil of its peel. The refreshing coolness of the lake we lived by was a sanctuary, washing away the grime and sweat of a full day of play. The mouth-watering aroma of freshly baked bread, pies, and cakes cooling on the window sill filled our noses with bliss and our bellies with hunger.

I loved to go to the park and swing as high as I could. The exhilaration of the breeze blowing through my hair, the wind caressing my face, the thrill of leaping off at the peak of the swing, momentarily experiencing the sensation of flight—these are some of the memories that have stayed with me, lighting up the darker corners of my past.

As I reflect upon those memorable days of my youth, I can't help but wonder—where did those times go?

The hot summers, the cool winters, the friends I thought would be forever—all seem to have vanished into the mists of time.

Yet, I've come to understand that happiness is not just a figment of our dreams, but a gift to be treasured every day. Life, despite its challenges of abuse, neglect, abandonment, fear, and doubt also offers beautiful moments, cherished memories, and opportunities for love and trust.

The key to navigating this journey lies in maintaining balance, learning to let go when necessary, and fostering an attitude of gratitude. It's about finding light amidst darkness and becoming a beacon of hope for others.

Choose Love

In the grand scheme of life, it is the choices you make daily that shape your destiny. It isn't so much the circumstances you find yourself in that hold importance, but rather, how you choose to deal with these situations. As a child, amidst the whirlwind of dysfunction that was my reality, I chose to cultivate a spirit of positivity and acceptance, rather than focusing on what was wrong.

 Some of my fondest memories were of those moments when my siblings and I managed to have some fun while navigating the disorder that surrounded us. I share these treasured recollections with you, hoping that they might inspire you to revisit your own cherished memories.

The way that I navigated the turbulent waters of my dysfunctional family life was by finding balance. I learned to cherish the moments of love and normalcy amidst the chaos.

Families, in all their varied forms, are crucibles where love and trauma are forged, shaping us into the individuals we become. Though there were few instances of love and positivity, we cherished those moments. One of my favorite memories was the Friday night ritual my siblings and I had. We would gather by the TV set, and one of the older kids would adjust the antenna ears to get better reception so we could watch Shock Theater with Elvira while eating popcorn. Some of the shows were really scary, but it was something that we looked forward to every week.

Another of my favorite memories was at Thanksgiving time, as it was a time when many of our cousins and relatives would all get together to celebrate the things we were grateful for. The adults would cook the various dishes that were everybody's favorites. The kids would be outside playing different games and getting caught up with each other's lives since the last time we saw each other. Of course, we each had our favorite cousins and would spend more time with them. This became my favorite time of the year. I loved the food and fun of spending time with my cousins.

My earliest memories were when we lived in Bethlehem, Pennsylvania. My mother worked at the Rodda/Born Candy Company where they made the Peeps candy. She worked the graveyard shift while my father was home with the four of us. This was after he got out of the Army.

One stormy night, I recall that the power went out and we were scared of the thunder and lightning, especially in the dark. Our father somehow managed to get us all into the kitchen area and, knowing where the candles were, he was able to get a couple lit for us. We were all huddled together with blankets and quilts when one of us knocked over a candle that quickly ignited the tablecloth into huge flames. I remember our father grabbing the candle and the tablecloth with his bare hands trying to put the flames out. Grabbing one of the quilts, he was able to smother the flames until they went out. He received some burns on his hands and arms. The rest of us were very lucky that we didn't get burned. His quick actions saved us from getting seriously hurt and the house from burning down. Our mother was very upset with him even though it wasn't his fault.

Our father had a gambling addiction that affected our parents' relationship and our family's finances in a very devastating way. We went from living in a beautiful two-story home with two of the nicest housekeepers, Mrs. White and Mrs. Plummer; who treated us like we were royalty. I still have fond memories of the time we spent together.

However, after a year or so, my father's gambling would cost us this home. I remember as a child saying goodbye to these sweet ladies who were like family. It was a very sad day for me and I never saw them again. After all of the highs and lows with our father's gambling and infidelity issues, my mother gave my father an ultimatum, "Settle down or else move on." He decided to work more and gamble less. It was my mother that convinced my father to join the Army in the first place. This would turn out to be a blessing in disguise for him. When he got older and could no longer take care of himself, the benefits he received from his service to this country became a lifesaver for him.

My mother and father stayed together for many years. Periodically, my father would leave and come back just long enough to get my mother pregnant. Then he'd leave again. Finally, after having six children, my parents called it quits for good. Both had their issues with infidelity. My father continued to gamble his money away, not giving my mother any child support, and eventually, he permanently abandoned us. This only escalated the various types of abuse we were subjected to.

As time passed, my parents' hatred for each other grew. They blamed each other for having so many kids. We were just the unwanted pieces in their dysfunctional game.

I recall once, during a heated argument with my mother, how she threatened my oldest brother with one of her favorite sayings to us kids: "I brought you into this world, and I can take you out."

Having heard this too many times, my oldest brother, with tears in his eyes, angrily screamed at her and said, "I didn't ask to be born."

Her response to him was, "I should have flushed you down the toilet when I had you.""

I could never be what she wanted me to be no matter how hard I tried.

It reminds me of one of the lyrics in one of my son Alexander Ergas's songs: "I can't be what you want me to be right now." from the song; "Not What You Want, but Stay."

In my case, it was never being able to please her. This was another one of the many ways she made us feel unwanted. I felt the fear, pain, and sadness that he was experiencing rushing through my mind and body. The two of us shared the painful memories of trauma and the bonds of protection and brotherly love.

Over time, I have tried my best to understand the stress my mother was under, later finding out that she was abused in so many of the same ways that we were. With trauma and not having any support from my father, she was grieving herself. There is no excuse for abuse, but I often wonder what our life as well as hers would have been like had she not been under so much stress; with the grief and suffering she had endured.

I am convinced that while our family experiences contribute significantly to who we are, they do not define us. Rather, they serve as stepping stones, guiding us toward the person we are destined to be. Sometimes parents can only show love the way they were shown love. It's the only thing they understand. This can take on many forms, like tough love, etc.

I have chosen to focus on those few moments of fun and peace when thinking about my parents. They both had some good qualities; both were great singers, dancers and could play instruments. My mother was very protective and was a great cook. My father had a good sense of humor and was a great artist. Despite the abuse I suffered at the hands of my parents, the healing work I have done has helped me to forgive them. Spiritual healing through love and forgiveness is the key that unlocks the heart where traumas can be released. Without forgiveness, compassion, and love, you cannot heal the past and embrace the future.

Now is the time to begin your journey. Good Luck and God Bless!

By sharing my experiences and coping mechanisms, I hope to encourage you to reconnect with your family, friends, or loved ones. Perhaps you, too, can let go of past fears and doubts that have held you back, and embrace love and trust as you chart your path forward.

My Hope For You

In the quiet whispers of our souls, we find an unparalleled sense of fulfillment and healing.

One of the most profound experiences I've been privileged to partake in is the act of attuning my ears to the gentle echoes of my Higher Self. This divine entity within me has served as a balm, soothing and nurturing my Inner Child who still bears the wounds of childhood trauma.

This sacred communion takes place in what I have previously described as the Healing Space, that ethereal realm where the conscious mind meets the spiritual self. It's there, in that space of infinite wisdom and knowledge, that I have embarked on a journey of healing that permeates every level of my soul. This is not a one-time event, but a continuous process, a pilgrimage towards wholeness and tranquility that I am still undertaking with each passing moment.

As you venture beyond the confines of this book, leaving behind the inked pages and stepping into the vast expanses of your own reality, my earnest prayer for you is to harness the transformative power of love.

I implore you to let love be your guide, your beacon as it unveils the exquisite beauty of your unique situation. It's challenging to give love when you don't feel loved. As you heal childhood wounds, the love inside you will grow, and you will experience positive relationship changes.

Remember, healing is not just a possibility but a divine right available to you. You have the power to transcend the shadows of your past and rise above the trauma that once held you captive. The peace, joy, and wisdom that your Higher Self has in store for you are not elusive dreams, but attainable realities.

Let your journey be one of discovery and transformation, of shedding old skins and embracing new beginnings. And in this journey, may you truly come to know, appreciate, and embody the profound wisdom your Higher Self has to offer. Remember the lyrics of two of my favorite Beatles songs, "All You Need is Love, Love is All You Need", and "Love is All, Love is You." Lennon & McCartney. **So What's Love Got To Do With It? Everything.**

Experiment with the challenges and solutions below to help you move forward on your healing journey. These are similar to others mentioned in earlier chapters, yet are worth repeating due to their importance. Here you will take a deeper dive into them. It's impossible to fully embrace love without the right mindset. Repetition helps you to remember things more deeply.

6 Transformational Challenges:	Solutions:
Facing your past traumas.	Moving beyond blame.
Finding your true self.	Self-love & acceptance.
Letting go of unhealthy habits.	Creating new ones.
Embracing self-confidence.	Honoring yourself.
Loving yourself unconditionally.	Focusing on your strengths.
Living your best life.	Forgiveness & Gratitude.

1. When dealing with past trauma, it can be challenging to let go of painful memories from those who have wronged you. Understandably, you often get caught up with the blaming aspect of the trauma. Here it is important to begin your journey with the right mindset; decide to do the work with a positive mindset no matter how challenging the process becomes. The goal of this journey is to free your wounded child from being stuck in the past. One solution that can be helpful, is learning to accept that the trauma happened, and release the need to blame, as it doesn't serve you to stay focused there. Those involved will be held accountable by their higher power, and justice will be satisfied; release those people to your Higher Power, and free yourself from the burden of carrying it any longer. Nobody is responsible for your actions as adults, yes they were sometimes when you were a kid, but now you have to let go of the past and move forward in love and trust. This process isn't as easy as it sounds, but when you decide to no longer allow this experience to hold you captive, and begin to let go of the blame and negative feelings, the healing process can begin. In some cases of serious abuse professional help is often needed.

2. To find your true self, you have to do a complete inventory of what your core values are; along with identifying the things that you hold as absolute truths in every cell of your being. One of the best ways to do this is by beginning to focus on yourself instead of everyone else. Often in life, you spend so much of your time focusing on others, that you don't have time to identify and satisfy your own needs. In other words, you must provide yourself with the things that you need to help with your healing process and journey. This can include becoming your own best friend, parent, sibling, etc. The focus is on accepting what has transpired in the past, acknowledging where you are in the present, and where

you want to be in the future. Do the things you feel good about, surround yourself with the people who support you, and help you to become the person you want to be. Embrace the new you with a sense of empowerment, love, and gratitude for your healing journey.

3. Sometimes letting go of unhealthy habits can be a daunting task, as many people in our lives encourage some of these behaviors. I remember a friend of mine struggling with alcohol addiction, trying his best to get sober, and after getting the help he needed; his wife at the time would drink in front of him, and encourage him to continue drinking, it was a futile effort for him; he eventually divorced her, and got back on track, and has been sober ever since. We have to stay away from those old habits, places, people and things that steer us back onto the same path. One of the best ways to let go of unhealthy habits is to get the help you need from professionals trained in the field of addiction. One of the best solutions for getting rid of them is to create new healthier habits to replace the old unhealthy ones. Make a list of the ones you want to do away with and some solutions for creating new ones to replace them with. For example, instead of drinking too much soda, try replacing it with flavored water that isn't full of sugar and carbonation. Making healthier food choices, exercising more, getting more sleep, creating an attitude of gratitude, smiling, laughing, and finding ways to have more fun and excitement in your life, if too self-centered, find ways to serve others, etc. Doing the opposite of what you are challenged with, sometimes is the answer you need to create a new habit; strive to do it for at least 21 to 30 days so it becomes a habit, if it doesn't stick at first, never give up, try it again until it works. If you can't do it on your own, get professional help.

4. Self-confidence is important for all of us as without it, the minute

some judgment or criticism comes our way, we sometimes fall apart. You need to feel special with the contributions you make when functioning in life. One of the best ways to do this is by honoring yourself. To do this, you need to identify your core values and beliefs, recognize your importance, and embrace your truths and desires about life. As Shakespeare said; "To thine own self be true." Many people in life try to make others feel bad about themselves, this is where knowing your true self changes the playing field. Always believe in yourself, let the Dream-Stealers, Nay-Sayer's, and Energy-Vampire's words; be like water rolling off your back when taking a shower. You honor others when you honor yourself. In the long run, those who are jealous of you will fade away as they watch you rise above the negativity and succeed simply by honoring yourself.

5. Sometimes you are harder on yourself than anybody else. During these times you have to learn to embrace your unconditional love and quit beating yourself up because you make mistakes. Nobody is perfect, everyone makes mistakes, learn from them, try not to repeat them, and love yourself through them. One of the best ways to do this is to focus on your strengths. This enables you to steer your focus and energies away from yourself. Despite your weaknesses, you can turn them into strengths. Love yourself anyway and look at them as opportunities to learn and grow. I often hear people putting themselves down by saying things like I don't like my nose, I hate my big feet, my hair is too thin, my body looks terrible, etc. There are some things about you that you cannot change, and should not change; while there are some things you can change for the good, and if it helps you feel better about yourself, so be it.

Ex: I knew a girl who hated her nose, so she got a nose job. After doing so, she hates her new nose and wishes that she hadn't changed it, and now it's too late. How many people have regretted plastic surgery after the fact? Many people have said that they liked their looks better before they changed them. Yet, others are happier with the changes they made, either way. Loving yourself unconditionally is important as you are worth being loved just the way you are. If you don't love yourself unconditionally, it's very difficult for others to love you without putting conditions on their love. By focusing on what's right about yourself, and maximizing your strengths it will be easier for you to receive the type of love you seek.

6. For guidance in living your best life, follow the five transformational challenges listed above and embrace the solutions for them. Along with those, I have found that Forgiveness and Gratitude are two of the most important catalysts that give Love its healing power. When you are open to forgiving others, and asking for forgiveness; the magical transformative power of love begins the process of decreasing the fears, doubts, and traumas of your past and replacing them with faith, trust, and a newfound hope of healing. This allows you to begin the process of living your best life.

When you try your best to let go, embrace change, and move forward, and nothing seems to work; try something different- Professional Counseling, Coaching, or Energy Healing. I have used all of the tools, tips, and techniques listed in this book with great results; and at times sought guidance from other professionals. I hope that you will find these to be as helpful for you as they have been for me.

What's Love got to do with It? (Everything, because without love you have nothing).

Here are some additional resources that might help you on your

healing journey.

What Happened To You? (Conversations On Trauma, Resilience, And Healing) By Bruce D. Perry, MD. PhD. & Oprah Winfrey.

Nourishing Your Soul (A Guided Imagery for Letting Go) Catherine Baer, MS, MS, LPC.

Build the Life You Want (The Art and Science of Getting Happier) By Arthur C. Brooks and   Oprah Winfrey.

The Family (A Revolutionary Way of Self-Discovery). John Bradshaw

Positivity (Top-Notch Research Reveals the Upward Spiral That Will Change Your Life). Barbara L. Fredrickson, PH.D.

The Loving Parent Guidebook (The solution to becoming your own parent). By the Adult Children of Alcoholics/Dysfunctional Families.

The Artist's Way by (The Spiritual Path to Higher Creativity). Julia Cameron

Happy For No Reason (7 Steps to Being Happy from the Inside Out). Marci Shimoff

Men Are From Mars, Women Are From Venus.   John Gray PhD.

Burnout (The Secret to Unlocking the Stress Cycle). Amelia Nagoski, DMA.

Talk To Me Like I'm Someone You Love (Relationship Repair In A Flash) Nancy Dreyfus

"Turn The Lights Back On" Billy Joel (This song will tug at your heart strings and inspire you to never give up.)

"Flowers" Miley Cyrus (This song shares a powerful message about loving yourself when things don't always work out in a relationship.)

"The Gifts of Imperfection" Brene Brown (Valuable insight on how as humans, we are hardwired for connection.)

"Coat of Many Colors" Dolly Parton

(This song reminds us of the power of gratitude and love.)

Being Seen, My Journey To Self-Love by Katie Myers
(This book helps you to recognize and manage the internal struggles that keep you at war with yourself).

Final Words
of Encouragement:

With all the craziness of my family life, there was light at the end of the tunnel. I'd like to share with you the closure I had with both of my parents, and a new beginning with my daughter Nicole.

Let's begin with my father. As a child and even into my teen and adult years, I blamed my mother for divorcing my father. She claimed that she divorced him because of his gambling addiction and infidelity. I had always believed that she drove him away because of how mean she was. It made sense to me with what I witnessed…she was the one I saw hitting him over the head with a cast iron skillet. My sister was later able to confirm through paperwork she found that he divorced her. I'm sure the responsibility for their divorce lies somewhere in the middle. He had gambling and infidelity issues; she had anger and infidelity issues. The truth is they were not a good match. They would often-break up and then get back together again. I asked him one day why he abandoned us and never helped to support us. He said it was because he could barely support himself, much less six kids. I felt like his reply was a lame excuse, but I have since forgiven him. Most of my memories of him were positive. The last time we spoke I made him laugh as I so often did. It was our way of connecting. It was never a secure attachment for me, but I find it interesting how in my need for a bond with my father, I told myself it was better than nothing. Not long after that conversation, he fell, and due to complications from it, he passed away. Both of my parents died due to complications from falls. I am grateful that we shared a love of music and languages.

I held greater animosity towards my mother because she was so abusive. She was the villain in my life story for a long time. Once I went six years without speaking to her because of my anger toward her. After years of counseling, I decided to reach out to her to have a better relationship. We would talk on the phone and once in a great while I would take my family over to see her. I was trying to let go of the past, but it wasn't easy.

Years later I had a powerful dream about her. In it, I saw her fall and hurt herself badly which led to her death. Although she lived in Georgia at the time, in this dream, she was at my sister's house in Florida. The whole process of her fall and death was as clear as day in my sleeping state. I felt a great sense of urgency to warn her about falling. I felt scared because anytime I dream about someone dying, it comes true. I remember dreaming about my grandmother's death when I was only 10 years old, and it happened just the way I dreamed it.

When I awoke from the dream, I began to reminisce about the few good times I had with her, and felt sad that for so many years, we didn't have the best relationship. My therapist wife sensed the importance of what I had experienced and she handed me a nearby legal pad to capture my dream on paper. As I began to write down the thoughts of my dream, it became a four-page tribute to my mother and it was all positive. I felt a sense of urgency to share my thoughts with her, so I scheduled a visit and my wife and I went to see her.

Already frail and unable to move well on her own, my mother and I sat huddled side by side in her tiny kitchen. My wife and one of my sisters were there as I read her the pages I had written after my ultimately prophetic dream. After sharing my thoughts and most loving feelings with her, everyone's eyes were teary and time seemed to stand still. At that moment, I asked my mother to forgive me for holding on to all the anger, blame, and bitterness I'd held toward her. With an energy of what felt like Divine love, she turned to me and said, "Son, you are the only one of my children who has never disrespected me, and you have no reason to apologize." So many emotions coursed through me then and I continue to reflect on the part I played in our relationship throughout the years. It was at this last time I saw her in person that she also apologized to me for all the trauma that she had put us through. I felt the sincerity in her words. What a great healing experience it was for the four of us that day. The closure and healing we both so desperately needed had come to pass. She left her earthly body a couple of weeks later while in Florida at my sister's house. She had gone there to be with my sister and be near the ocean. Complications due to a fall just like in my dream would prevent her from making it to the ocean. I am forever grateful for the divine message sent to me in the dream that provided the opportunity for closure and healing. I love and miss my mother. She is still with us as our family remembers her great cooking, baking, and love of music and dance.

Reconnecting with my daughter Nicole-an answer to my prayers, has brought me great joy and happiness. After the many tears of reconnecting, I expressed to her my sorrow for missing out on all the important moments of her life. Her response, to my surprise, was to create a video of some of those special moments from her childhood, teen, and adult years for me. I wept as I watched her grow up before my very eyes. This is one of the kindest things that anyone has ever done for me. I couldn't be more proud of her and all that she has accomplished throughout the years. Her parents did a fantastic job of raising her, and I'm eternally thankful to them.

I love my wife and all my children. I am thankful for them, and proud of all they have and will accomplish in their lives. They have taught me more about love and forgiveness than I could've ever learned on my own. Catherine, Nicole, Ereca, Mikey, Alexander, and Zoe—you are God's greatest blessings in my life.

I believe that if you have an opportunity to forgive someone, you should take it. When you release the relationship challenges to a Higher Power, you can receive the kind of loving closure that can heal you at your deepest levels. This was my experience.

I would like to thank you personally for taking this healing journey with me. It has been an honor and a privilege for me to share many of my favorite tools, techniques, quotations, and stories with you. These have helped me and many of my family, friends, and patients with their healing process. It's my hope and prayer that you get something valuable from them. I know that if you apply these lessons to your own life, you will be inspired and motivated to get up one more time, and give life and love another chance. I have found that there are many ways to let go of the past traumas that sabotage our ability to love and be loved. One of the best ways to do it is to reconnect your Inner Child with your Higher Self, heal the past, and move forward into the present. I wish you the very best on your healing journey, and if you have any questions or are interested in coaching or energy healing for you or someone you know; feel free to contact me.

Please share this book with anyone you feel could benefit from the lessons contained in it, and look forward to some of my upcoming works. This book is just a footnote into my personal journey, look for the full story in the future. Please keep my mantra in mind as you motor through your day. I truly believe it will inspire and motivate you to keep moving forward when the going gets tough.

"The love that unfolds in front of you daily is perfect. Embrace it, honor it, give thanks for it, and most of all, share it because, out of our everyday random acts of kindness and love, a greater love for everyone and everything around us is born."

Good luck & God Bless.

~ Dr. Mitch Ergas

If you have any questions about the Book, Life-Coaching or Healing Programs, I can be reached at drergas.thehealingspace@gmail.com.

Meet the Author

Dr. Mitch Ergas, DC, ACN, CFMP has worked in the health and wellness industry for decades. Prior to his career as a Chiropractor, Nutritionist, and Certified Functional Medicine Practitioner, he served in various roles such as Hairdresser, Make-up Artist, Kung-Fu Teacher, Massage/Energy therapist, and Life-Coach. He's passionate about meeting people where they are and helping them get to where they want to go. With his combined set of skills, he's helped thousands of people throughout his career; and looks forward to helping many more in the future as he continues his own journey of becoming the best version of himself..

If you would like to learn more about his Coaching and Healing programs, please email: drergas.thehealingspace@gmail.com

www.ingramcontent.com/pod-product-compliance
Lightning Source LLC
LaVergne TN
LVHW081328060426
835513LV00012B/1224